Ranger Rick's NatureScope

POLLUTION
PROBLEMS & SOLUTIONS

National Wildlife Federation

LEARNING TRIANGLE PRESS

*Connecting
kids, parents, and teachers
through learning*

An imprint of McGraw-Hill
New York San Francisco Washington, D.C. Auckland Bogotá Caracas
Lisbon London Madrid Mexico City Milan Montreal New Delhi
San Juan Singapore Sydney Tokyo Toronto

Library of Congress Cataloging-in-Publication Data

Pollution: problems and solutions /National Wildlife Federation.
      p. cm.—(Ranger Rick's naturescope)
    ISBN 0-07-047105-3 (pbk.)
     1. Pollution 2. Pollution—Study and teaching—Activity
    programs. I. National Wildlife Federation II. Series.
    TD178.P65 1998
    372.3'57044—dc21   97-36214

McGraw-Hill

A Division of The McGraw·Hill Companies

CIP

1 2 3 4 5 6 7 8 9 JDL/JDL 9 0 3 2 1 0 9 8

ISBN 0-07-047105-3

NatureScope® was originally conceived by National Wildlife Federation's School Programs Editorial Staff, under the direction of Judy Braus, Editor. Special thanks to all of the Editorial Staff, Scientific, Educational Consultants and Contributors who brought this series of eighteen publications to life.

NATIONAL WILDLIFE FEDERATION EDITORIAL STAFF
Creative Services Manager: Sharon Schiliro
Editor, Ranger Rick® magazine: Gerry Bishop
Director, Classroom-related Programs: Margaret Tunstall
Contributors: Patti Aronson, Nancy Carter, Carol J. Boggis,
Ann Hardison, and Timothy Donahue

McGRAW-HILL EDP STAFF
Acquisitions Editor: Judith Terrill-Breuer
Editorial Supervisor: Patricia V. Amoroso
Production Supervisor: Claire Stanley
Designer: York Production Services
Cover Design: David Saylor

McGraw-Hill books are available at special quantity discounts to use as premiums and sales promotions, or for use in corporate training programs. For more information, please write to the Director of Special Sales, McGraw-Hill, 11 West 19th Street, New York, NY 10011. Or contact your local bookstore.

Printed and bound by the John D. Lucas Printing Company. This book is printed on recycled and acid-free paper.

TM and ® designate trademarks of National Wildlife Federation and are used, under license, by The McGraw-Hill Companies, Inc.

RRNS

OTHER TITLES IN *RANGER RICK'S NATURESCOPE*

GOAL

Ranger Rick's NatureScope is a creative education series dedicated to inspiring in children an understanding and appreciation of the natural world while developing the skills they will need to make responsible decisions about the environment.

TABLE OF CONTENTS

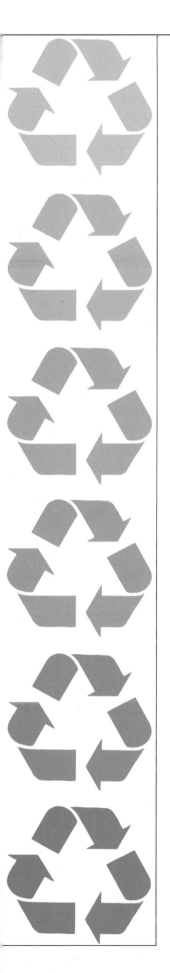

ABOUT THE ISSUE

AGE GROUPS
Primary (grades K-2)
Intermediate (grades 3-5)
Advanced (grades 6-8)

OUTDOOR ACTIVITIES
Outdoor activities are marked with this
symbol:

COPYCAT PAGES
Copycat Pages are ready-to-copy
activity sheets that supplement the
activities. Look at the bottom of each
Copycat Page for the name and page
number of the activity it goes with.

POLLUTION—NO EASY ANSWERS

A haze of thick smog. An oil spill. An overflowing landfill. It's not hard to find examples of pollution in our society. But it is hard to define exactly what pollution is. For example, is a can tossed on the ground pollution? How about an unsightly billboard? The noise from a nearby airport?

According to experts, all of these examples can be types of pollution. Broadly defined, pollution is any human-caused change in the environment that creates an undesirable effect on living and nonliving things. Most types of pollution cause some type of physical harm. But some don't. Noise, for example, often creates more psychological damage than physical damage, but it's still considered a type of pollution. In short, pollution is bad stuff—for the environment and for people and other living things.

From Manure to Monoxide: For thousands of years, pollution wasn't much of a problem. As long as people lived in scattered settlements and the world's human population was relatively small, the earth's natural systems could accommodate the effects of human waste. But once people began to live in cities and to invent machines and synthetic chemicals, pollution started taking its toll. Pollution has been linked to the fall of Rome (lead in the pipes); the cholera epidemic in 19th-century London (garbage in the streets); and many other significant events throughout history.

Though pollution has been around for thousands of years, the sources of our pollution problems have changed, and the amount of pollution has increased dramatically. A century ago, people were dealing with pollution from animal waste, coal ash, and open dumps. Today, pesticides, fertilizers, radiation, carbon monoxide, acid rain, and a host of other "new" and toxic pollutants are the troublemakers. This increase in the amount, number, and toxicity of pollutants, combined with an ever-increasing human population, has made pollution worse than ever before—threatening the very integrity of earth's life-support systems.

Hard to Pin Down: In this issue, we focus on air, water, and land pollution. However, in many cases the categories overlap. For example, pesticides can contaminate air, water, and land, depending on how they are manufactured, used, and disposed of. Many pollutants also travel great distances and can change form, making it hard to pin down exactly where they came from.

The effects of pollution can also be hazy. For one thing, pollutants can affect different people in different ways. People with respiratory problems and allergies, for example, are often more sensitive to air pollution than people without these problems. And it's often hard to tie adverse health effects to specific types of pollution. In general, pollution can cause serious and immediate problems, such as injury or death, as well as chronic, long-term problems that can take years to surface.

Pollution does more than affect human health. It also limits our activities, harms wildlife and habitat, defaces buildings, and has the potential to disrupt the planet's natural systems, including global climate patterns.

No Single Cause: Almost every human activity—from how we get around to how we grow our crops—creates some type of pollution. And a combination of factors, from economics to politics to ethics, further complicates pollution problems. (For more about the causes of air, water, and land pollution, see the background information in each chapter.)

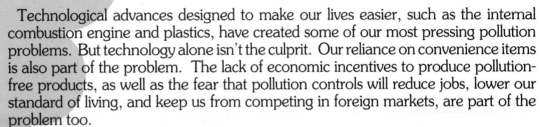

Technological advances designed to make our lives easier, such as the internal combustion engine and plastics, have created some of our most pressing pollution problems. But technology alone isn't the culprit. Our reliance on convenience items is also part of the problem. The lack of economic incentives to produce pollution-free products, as well as the fear that pollution controls will reduce jobs, lower our standard of living, and keep us from competing in foreign markets, are part of the problem too.

Not understanding the consequences of pollution is also part of the problem. For years, people thought that they could safely get rid of garbage, sewage, exhaust, and other waste products by throwing them away, flushing them down the drain, or releasing them into the air. But we're now realizing that the waste we dispose of can come back to haunt us in a variety of forms.

Poverty and Pollution: Pollution is intrinsically linked to social problems, such as poverty and overpopulation. In many cases, people on limited incomes cannot just move away from a chemical dump site or a smog-filled city. They can't afford to drink bottled water or pay for organically grown vegetables. The struggle to simply survive forces them to take risks that others can afford to avoid. And when poverty is combined with the pressures of overpopulation, which it often is, both pollution and poverty are exacerbated.

Weighing the Risks: We know that some pollution will always exist. But how much pollution is acceptable? What are the short- and long-term risks of a polluted environment to individuals, communities, and society as a whole? To deal with questions like these, policymakers are starting to rely on a relatively new and imprecise process called *risk assessment*. Risk assessment helps people understand and quantify the risks posed by using certain technologies and not using others, including the probability and severity of the risks. But determining and evaluating risks is often extremely difficult. In many cases, data on the risks involved with new technologies don't exist, and scientists must rely on computer models that have no proven reliability. And it's hard to quantify intangibles such as the loss of an endangered species or an ecologically pristine site. Even if risks can be calculated, risk assessment is controversial because some technologies benefit certain people while imposing risks on others.

A Question of Values: In the past, we've spent most of our efforts *cleaning up* pollution rather than *preventing* it. But experts are now looking more to reducing the pollution we produce in the first place. In the long run, preventing pollution saves money, protects resources, prevents health problems, and improves the overall quality of life. But making the decision to prevent pollution involves more than politics, economics, and health. It also involves values. Taking into account both short- and long-term risks, people must rely on their own value systems to decide how important it is to prevent pollution now—for themselves, for their neighbors, for society as a whole, and for future generations.

Pollution Patrol

Go on a scavenger hunt to search for signs of pollution.

Objectives:
Define pollution. Describe several examples of pollution.

Ages:
Primary, Intermediate, and Advanced

Materials:
- *chalkboard or easel paper*
- *copies of clues on page 5*
- *magazines (optional)*
- *scissors (optional)*
- *glue (optional)*
- *construction paper (optional)*

Subjects:
Science and Social Studies

our kids can go on a "pollution patrol" scavenger hunt to look for different types of pollution and signs of potential pollution in their community.

Begin the activity by asking the kids what kinds of things come to mind when they think of pollution. List their ideas on a chalkboard or sheet of easel paper. Then use the background information on pages 2-3 to explain what pollution is. Ask the kids if they want to add any other examples to their list or delete any that they suggested before.

Next tell the group that they will be going outside to look for some of the types of pollution that you talked about. Tell the kids to be on the lookout for signs of pollution in the air, in water, and on land. They should also keep noise pollution in mind.

FOR YOUNGER KIDS

Before taking the group outside, show the kids examples of pollution "evidence" they might find on their scavenger hunt. You might bring in things such as an empty beverage can, some litter from a fast-food restaurant, an empty container of household cleaner, and other examples of trash. Or you could show pictures of cars, smokestacks, outdoor grills, and so on to give the kids ideas about what to look for.

Once you're outside, tell the kids that they should rely on their senses to help them locate and identify pollution. For example, they might smell exhaust from nearby cars,

see oil spots on the road, or hear noise from a plane taking off or flying overhead. You may want to have the children work in teams, with each team focusing on just one form of pollution. For example, different teams could search for pollution they can see, hear, or smell. Or they could search for pollution that's on land, in water, or in the air. Each time someone comes across a different kind of pollution, stop to discuss where it might have come from and what effect it might have on wildlife and the environment. (See "What Makes It Pollution?" on the next page for some ideas.)

FOR OLDER KIDS

Before going outside, use the pollution examples in **bold** type under "What Makes It Pollution?" on the next page to make up a scavenger hunt clue sheet. Then pass out a copy of the clue sheet to each person. Explain to the kids that they can work in pairs to try to look for the signs of pollution listed on their clue sheets. They can also add signs they find that aren't included in their scavenger hunt list.

Now take the kids outside. Tell them to think about whether each type of pollution they find affects air, land, water, or some combination of the three. Also tell them to think about whether each type of pollution affects people or wildlife in some way.

When the kids have finished their walk, go over the list. Have the kids take turns describing where they saw various signs, and then discuss the likely sources of pollution and the possible consequences. Use the information under "What Makes It

Pollution?" to help with the discussion. (You might also want to read through the background information in chapters two, three, and four for more detailed information about the effects of pollution.)

If there aren't many signs of pollution in your immediate area, have the kids look for them around their neighborhood or on their way to and from your meeting area. Or have them do their scavenger hunt inside by searching for the clues in magazines. They can work in small teams to cut out pictures and make pollution collages. Tell them that they can include examples of things that could contribute to pollution even though the picture may not show the pollution itself. For example, a picture of laundry detergent or a washing machine could symbolize the fact that many kinds of detergent contain phosphates—chemicals that can pollute surface water and groundwater. Or the kids might include a cigarette

ACTION TIP!

OPERATION

CLEANUP

Have your kids plan a community cleanup campaign, using what they found out about pollution in their community. For example, they could follow up their scavenger hunt with a litter pickup project. And for problems that are more difficult to solve, such as local problems with air and water pollution, the kids could write letters, work on a pollution fact-finding mission, or help educate others about pollution in the community. To help them get started, try "Clean Up Your Act!" on page 72.

ad and describe how cigarettes can contribute to the problem of indoor air pollution. (For more about indoor air pollution, see page 35.) When they have finished, have the teams present their collages to the rest of the group.

WHAT MAKES IT POLLUTION?

(*Note:* This list does not include all the problems related to each entry. For example, there are a number of pollution problems related to plastic foam, but we've included only those related *directly* to plastic foam *litter*.)

oil stains on pavement: rain can wash oil into water supplies

aluminum beverage can: unsightly; doesn't biodegrade; sharp edges may injure wildlife or people; small creatures may get trapped inside

paper litter: unsightly; inks and bleaching chemicals can contaminate soil and water

plastic six-pack ring: unsightly; doesn't biodegrade; may strangle wildlife

litter in a pond, lake, stream, or other body of water: unsightly; may injure aquatic animals that get stuck in litter or try to eat it

lawn-care truck: lawn-care products contain chemicals that may harm wildlife, pets, and people; rain can wash chemicals into water supplies

USDA—Soil Conservation Service

construction site: noise may be annoying and may damage hearing of construction workers; construction dust may pollute air; rain can wash uncovered soil into surface water; creates solid and hazardous waste

car, truck, or bus exhaust: pollutes air; harms human health; may contribute to global climate change

storm drain: rain washes litter, soil, chemicals, and other pollutants into the drain, which carries pollutants into surface water

animal waste: rain can wash waste into water supplies; can harm human health

household chemical container: unsightly; can leak harmful chemicals into soil, water, or air

jet or airplane noise: annoying; may damage hearing of people who live near or work at airports

smog: harms human health

overflowing trash container: unsightly; litter may trap or choke wildlife

traffic noise: annoying

glass litter: unsightly; broken glass may injure people or wildlife; small creatures may get trapped inside jars or bottles

smokestack: releases pollutants into air

aerosol spray can: may contain air-polluting propellants or chemicals that can harm people or wildlife

plastic foam litter: unsightly; doesn't biodegrade; may injure animals that mistake bits of plastic for food

discarded tires: unsightly; may catch on fire and release harmful pollutants into soil, water, or air

roadside dump: unsightly; may contain hazardous materials that can leak into soil, water, or air; different types of materials may harm wildlife in different ways (poisoning, choking, trapping, and so on)

smoke from a chimney: pollutes air; may contribute to global climate change

gasoline pump: nozzle releases toxic fumes; underground storage tank may leak gasoline into water supplies

person spraying garden pesticide: chemicals may harm people or pets; may kill species other than the targeted pests; rain can wash chemicals into water supplies

candy or gum wrapper: unsightly; foil and plastic doesn't biodegrade

bare soil on a slope: rain can wash soil into surface water

Pollution Hot Spots

Use geography clues to map major pollution events. Research and map some other pollution events.

Objectives:
Describe several significant pollution events. Find where they happened on a world map.

Ages:
Intermediate and Advanced

Materials:
• *copies of page 12*
• *atlases*
• *large world map*
• *slips of paper*

Subjects:
Geography, Social Studies, and History

ociety has become increasingly dependent on a long list of chemicals and other materials that seemingly have made everyday life easier. But industrial accidents, waste created from processing hazardous materials, and the materials themselves can contribute to pollution problems. Try this activity to help your group learn about some pollution mishaps around the world, as well as some of the positive events that have helped solve pollution problems.

Before you get started, gather some atlases so the kids in each of several small groups can share one. They'll need to refer to a world map, a map of the U.S. that shows state borders, a map of North America, and a map of Eurasia. Also copy each of the "Pollution News Tips" listed below onto a slip of paper.

PART 1: FOLLOW THE REPORTER

Begin the activity by dividing the group into teams of four or five kids and giving an atlas to each team. Then tell the kids they'll be reading entries from a fictional reporter's journal to find out about some of the world's major pollution events.

Pass out copies of page 12 and have the kids read the journal entries. Then tell the teams to use the maps in their atlases, along with the geography clues in each journal entry, to identify where each pollution event took place. Be sure they note whether they must identify a country, state, or city.

(Depending on the geography skills of your group, you may want to provide the answers in mixed-up order along with the clues. You might also want to go over some of the unfamiliar concepts.)

After the kids finish, go over the page using the answers below. You may want to discuss the events, both positive and negative. Also have the kids consider how the negative events, though sometimes tragic, can help people learn to avoid similar events in the future.

PART 2: MAPPING POLLUTION

Have some kids make labels that identify the events they learned about in Part 1. Then have other kids attach the labels to a large world map. For example, they could mark London on the map with a label that includes the place, date, and a brief description of the "killer fog" event.

Next pass out the slips of paper you made earlier and have the kids work in pairs to research these other important pollution events. Then have them mark these events on the map too. Also have the kids watch for newspaper and magazine articles describing pollution-related events. They can continue adding these to their pollution map to keep it up-to-date. Your group may also want to follow local pollution issues, and chart local events on a state map.

ANSWERS: 1—London, 2—Japan, 3—New York City, 4—Mexico, 5—Switzerland, 6—Canada, 7—Florida, 8—Ethiopia, 9—Brazil

---

POLLUTION NEWS TIPS

Torrey Canyon; oil spill; Mar 18, 1967
Cuyahoga River; caught fire; Jun 22, 1969
DDT; banned due, in part, to effects on bird populations; 1972
PCBs; publicity about effects of these chemicals in Great Lakes; 1976
Argo Merchant; oil spill; 1976
Love Canal; evacuation of community built on toxic waste dump; 1978
Amoco Cadiz; oil spill; Mar 16, 1978
Three Mile Island; nuclear power plant accident; Mar 28, 1979

Times Beach; dioxin in soil; Dec 31, 1982
Bhopal; chemical plant accident; Dec 3, 1984
Agent Orange; publicity about effects of toxic chemical used in Vietnam War; 1984
ozone hole; discovery announced; May 1985
Chernobyl; nuclear power plant accident; Apr 26, 1986
garbage barge (*Mobro*); garbage crisis; 1987
medical waste; washed up on East Coast beaches; summer 1988
Exxon Valdez; oil spill; Mar 24, 1989

Car Talk

Learn about the pollution problems associated with cars by making a car flip-up or bulletin board.

Objectives:
Identify several pollution problems associated with cars. Discuss some ways to cut down on these problems.

Ages:
Intermediate and Advanced

Materials:
- *copies of page 13*
- *scissors*
- *tape*
- *colored pencils or markers*
- *construction paper*
- *glue (optional)*
- *magazines (optional)*
- *reference books (optional)*

Subjects:
Science and Social Studies

Can't live with them; can't live without them. Although they provide individual freedom for millions of people and jobs for one out of ten workers in the U.S., cars are one of the worst sources of pollution around. Here's an activity that will get your group thinking about the many ways cars contribute to pollution and how people may be able to cut down on the problems cars cause.

To start, read the "Car Clues" listed below to the kids and have them try to figure out what object the clues are referring to. After they discover that the clues are referring to cars, pass out a copy of page 13 to each person. Tell the kids that each square on the bottom half of the page contains facts that relate to one of the car characteristics pictured on the top of the page. Then give the kids time to figure out which group of facts go with each picture. (You may want to give the kids some time to do research to find out more about each car characteristic.) Have the kids indicate their answers by writing the car characteristic titles in the blanks on the corresponding fact squares.

Afterward go over their answers and use the information under "Auto Awareness" (see page 8) to discuss the ways cars contribute to pollution. (Refer to chapters two, three, and four for more details about different forms of air, water, and land pollution.) Follow up by having the kids brainstorm some possible solutions to the problems they discussed. Go over what they come up with, using the information under "Some Solutions" on page 8. Then have the kids follow the directions below to make a flip-up showing car problems and solutions.

Older kids may want to use the Copycat Page and flip-up instructions as a guide to create an "auto awareness" bulletin board. They can do some research to find out about other problems that cars cause, such as habitat destruction, wildlife road kills, accidents, and so on. The kids can use their bulletin board to help educate others about the problems that cars cause and ways to solve the problems.

MAKE AN AUTO FLIP-UP

1. Color the pictures on the top half of page 13, and then cut the squares apart along the dashed lines.
2. Draw, or cut out from a magazine, a picture of a car. Tape the top edge of the car to the middle of a piece of construction paper.
3. Cut apart the fact squares and tape or glue them around the car.
4. Tape each picture square on top of its matching fact square. Make sure you tape *only* the top edge of each picture so you can lift it up to see the facts underneath.
5. Flip up the car picture and write some solutions to car-caused pollution problems underneath it.

CAR CLUES

- Americans throw away enough of them every 20 minutes to form a stack as high as the Empire State Building.
- During 1989, more than 35 million of them were made throughout the world.
- They add millions of tons of carbon dioxide to the atmosphere each year.
- Worldwide, they burned over 200 billion gallons of gasoline in 1986.

(continued next page)

ACTION TIP!

EDUCATE OTHERS

Have the kids make posters outlining some of the problems that cars create and ways individuals can help solve these problems. Then get permission to display the posters in community centers, grocery stores, and other central locations.

Car Manufacturing

- Mining for raw materials such as bauxite (to make aluminum) or iron ore (to make steel) creates waste that can pollute land and water. It also creates dust that pollutes the air and causes soil erosion that pollutes water when the soil washes into surface water.
- Processing raw materials into car parts causes pollution. Steel factories and other manufacturing plants, for example, create waste products that pollute air, land, and water.
- Many car parts are made of plastic—a product made from oil (see "Fossil Fuels").
- Auto assembly plants create waste, such as toxic paints and lubricants, that pollutes air, land, and water.

Junked Cars and Tires

- Each year, at least eight million cars end up in U.S. junkyards. Car junkyards are ugly and take up valuable land.
- When reusable materials aren't recovered after cars are junked, resources are wasted and new materials must be made from scratch (see "Car Manufacturing").
- Batteries, air conditioners, and other parts of junked cars can leak. The toxic materials they release can pollute water supplies or air.
- Tire dumps can sometimes catch on fire, releasing toxic fumes that pollute the air and toxic residues that can leach into water supplies. And tires dumped into landfills take up a lot of space.

USDA—Soil Conservation Service

Fossil Fuels

- Most cars run on gasoline, a product made from oil. Drilling, processing, and transporting oil creates air, water, and land pollution.
- When engines burn gasoline, they release toxic gases and other waste products into the air. These substances can cause respiratory diseases, cancer, and other health problems. They can also contribute to acid rain and global climate change.
- Car engines require motor oil. Just one quart of oil can contaminate thousands of gallons of water, polluting drinking water supplies and poisoning wildlife.
- Driving at excessive speeds cuts down on fuel efficiency.

Roads

- Building roads creates dust and waste, and causes soil erosion. All can pollute air, land, and water.
- Asphalt, a main ingredient used in making roads, is made from oil (see "Fossil Fuels").
- Increased traffic on roads creates noise pollution and increases air pollution from exhaust fumes.
- Road salt, used to melt ice and snow, washes off roads, damaging roadside vegetation and polluting water supplies.

Auto Air Conditioners

- Using car air conditioners can cause cars to burn more fuel.
- When junked or improperly maintained, car air conditioners can leak ozone-damaging CFCs into the atmosphere.

Car Care

- Washing cars can pollute waterways when detergent and road grime run into storm drains and then into surface water.
- Improperly inflated tires reduce fuel efficiency.
- Motor oil; brake, transmission, and window-washer fluids; antifreeze; and lubricants that leak or are disposed of improperly can pollute land and water.
- An improperly maintained engine doesn't burn fuel efficiently and can increase air pollution.

SOME SOLUTIONS

- Alternative power sources, such as sunlight, electricity, ethanol, and methane, can eliminate many of the pollution problems associated with burning fossil fuels.
- Recycling car parts can cut down on pollution caused by mining and processing new materials.
- Recycling CFCs and oil can prevent air and water pollution.
- Developing safer refrigerants can eliminate use of ozone-destroying CFCs.
- Engines and exhaust systems can be redesigned to burn fuel more efficiently and to reduce the emissions of air pollutants.
- Individuals can reduce auto-caused pollution by walking, biking, carpooling, or using public transportation; by not exceeding 55 mph on highways; by keeping cars well maintained; by using service stations that support recycling and reuse of materials; by supporting laws that require tighter pollution-control measures; and by buying fuel-efficient cars.

ANSWERS: A—5, B—2, C—6, D—1, E—4, F—3

Pollution Pursuits

Answer some pollution survey questions and play a pollution trivia game.

Objectives:
Discuss the connection between individual behavior and pollution. Describe several types of pollution and explain what causes each type. Explain how pollution affects people, wildlife, and the environment.

Ages:
Intermediate and Advanced

Materials:
* *copies of the survey questions on page 10*
* *trivia questions on pages 10-11*
* *slips of paper*
* *chalkboard or easel paper*
* *index cards cut into 3-inch squares*
* *sack*
* *drawing paper or mural paper*
* *crayons or markers*
* *tape*

Subjects:
Science and Social Studies

---

ere's an activity that you can use to kick off *and* wrap up a unit on pollution. In Part 1 you can find out what your kids know and think about pollution by having them take a short survey. Then, by playing a trivia game in Part 2, the kids can review what they've learned.

PART 1: THE SURVEY

Pass out a copy of the survey questions under "What Do You Think?" on page 10 to each person. Tell the group that the questions deal with different aspects of pollution, and that you'd like them to answer the questions as honestly as possible. Explain that you want to find out what they know and think about pollution, but reassure them that it's not a test. (Some of the questions are more difficult than others. Adapt them to fit the needs of your group.)

After the kids have completed the survey, collect their answers and the questions. Explain that they'll get a chance to discuss the answers later on. You can use the kids' answers to help you decide what to cover during your pollution study.

After completing your pollution studies, pass out the survey questions and have the kids answer them again. Then pass out their original responses and have the kids compare their answers. Ask them how their answers changed, if at all. Then discuss why they think their answers changed.

PART 2: WHAT'S YOUR POLLUTION IQ?

Your kids can play a team game that will help them review—and tie together—all they've learned about pollution. Here's how to set up and play the game:

Getting Ready

1. Write the numbers 1-52 on separate slips of paper and put the slips in a sack. Also include five slips with an "X" marked on each one and five slips with an "O" marked on each one.

2. Divide the group into three teams and give each team a sheet of drawing paper or mural paper and some crayons or markers. Assign one team to be air pollution, one to be water pollution, and one to be land pollution. Explain that, as a group, each team should draw a scene that is affected by the type of pollution they've been assigned. Tell them to make their drawings as detailed as they'd like and at least 11" X 17".

3. Copy the following list of pollutants on a chalkboard or sheet of easel paper. Have each team make two sets of pollutant cards by copying each of the pollutants listed under each team's name onto two separate 3-inch square cards. (There should be a total of 12 pollutant squares for each team.) Then have the kids on each team "pollute" their scene by taping the 12 pollutants on their drawing.

AIR: carbon dioxide, acid rain, CFCs, smog, particulates, carbon monoxide
WATER: lead, mercury, PCBs, animal waste, fertilizers, pesticides
LAND: radioactive waste, plastic, toxic ash, paper, metal, yard waste

4. Have each team pick a captain. Then have the teams hang their drawings where everyone can see them.

Playing the Game

Tell the kids that the object of the game is to get rid of all 12 pollutants from their scene. To do that, they'll have to correctly answer pollution questions. To play, have a person from the first team draw one of the numbered slips of paper from the sack. Then read the corresponding question listed under "Pollution Puzzlers" below. Only the team captain can answer, but he or she should confer with the rest of the team before giving an answer.

If team members answer the question correctly, they get to remove one or more of the pollutants from their scene. (Some of the questions indicate that a team can remove two pollutants.) If they answer incorrectly, the numbered slip of paper goes back in the sack. After one team has a turn, it's time for another team to pick a question and answer it. If team members pick a slip with an X, they have to put one pollutant back on their drawing (if they've lost one) and they don't get to answer a question. But if they pick a slip with an O, they get to take a pollutant off their drawing and then pick another question. You can play until one team has removed all 12 pollutants, or you can set a time limit and declare a winner when the time is up.

WHAT DO YOU THINK?

1. What is pollution? List five examples of pollution.
2. List some of the causes of pollution.
3. How do you contribute to pollution? Name three ways.
4. What are three things you could do to help reduce pollution?
5. Give some examples of how pollution affects living things and the environment.
6. Can pollution in one country harm people in another country? Explain your answer.
7. Do you think the United States creates more pollution than other countries? Explain your answer.

POLLUTION PUZZLERS

1. Which of the following is an example of pollution? Give all correct answers. (all)
   a. litter in a stream
   b. noise from a nearby airport
   c. cigarette smoke in a restaurant
   d. a billboard
   e. fishing line tangled around a log
2. Name three major pollution events that have occurred in the last decade. (*Exxon Valdez* oil spill; Chernobyl nuclear power plant explosion; *Mobro* garbage barge, and so on)
3. How does the world's increasing human population contribute to pollution problems? (more people means more hazardous materials; more garbage; more energy use, which contributes to pollution; and so on)
4. Give an example of noise pollution and explain how it can hurt people and other living things. (construction noise, noise from jets and motor vehicles, noise from stereos, and so on; can damage people's hearing, can disturb wildlife breeding and feeding activities)
5. Which pesticide caused a decrease in bald eagle populations following World War II? (DDT)
6. What is the connection between plastic foam and the ozone layer? (Some foam is made with CFCs, which deplete the ozone layer.)

7. True or false: Plants can help absorb indoor air pollution. (true)
8. What are fossil fuels? (coal, oil, and other fuels that formed millions of years ago from the remains of ancient plants and animals)
9. True or false: Air pollution inside buildings can sometimes be worse than air pollution outside. (true)
10. Name three things that contribute to indoor air pollution. (cigarette smoke; emissions from copy machines, art supplies, new carpeting and furniture; and so on)
11. Name two possible consequences of global climate change. (sea level rise, droughts, cooling or warming in some areas, extinction of some species of plants and animals)
12. What air pollutant is the main contributor to the greenhouse effect? (carbon dioxide)
13. [worth two pollutants] Name two ways that low-level ozone can affect people or the environment. (makes people's eyes and throats burn, damages crops and forests, makes rubber and other materials deteriorate faster than they normally would)
14. How does acid rain form? (pollutants released from power plants and motor vehicles combine with water droplets in the atmosphere and fall to earth as acid rain, fog, or snow)

15. Why is it important to protect the ozone layer? (to keep the amount of harmful ultraviolet radiation that reaches the earth from increasing, which would increase occurrences of skin cancer and affect plant growth)
16. How can deforestation contribute to global climate change? (the burning of forests releases more carbon dioxide into the air and also removes trees and other vegetation that would otherwise absorb carbon dioxide)
17. [worth two pollutants] Name three products that contain CFCs. (some aerosols, computer parts, coolants for refrigerators and air conditioners, many kinds of foam products)
18. How can cutting down on energy use help reduce air pollution? (reduced demand for electricity results in less coal or oil being burned in power plants, which results in less air pollution)
19. True or false: Air pollution is something you can always either see or smell. (false)
20. What is groundwater? (underground water that fills the spaces between soil particles and rocks)
21. What are some of the ways groundwater gets polluted? (leaking landfills, leaking hazardous waste sites, pesticides and other chemicals seeping through the soil, and so on)

22. The area of land that rain and snowmelt drain off of is called a _____. (watershed)

23. Toxic chemicals gushing out of a pipe into a river is an example of what kind of pollution: nonpoint or point pollution? (point pollution)

24. Pesticides, oil, and fertilizers washing into rivers from roads, fields, and farms is an example of what kind of pollution: nonpoint or point pollution? (nonpoint pollution)

25. More ocean oil pollution comes from: (b)
  a. large oil tanker spills
  b. routine cleaning of empty oil tankers

26. [worth two pollutants] Name four substances that can contaminate groundwater. (pesticides, road salt, motor oil, fertilizers, animal waste, gasoline, battery acids, and so on)

27. True or false: Wetlands can help purify water by absorbing harmful pollutants. (true)

28. Name two ways that plastic trash can harm wildlife. (when eaten, can block digestive system and cause starvation; can entangle or strangle birds and other animals)

29. What ingredient in laundry detergent can cause algae to grow much faster than normal? (phosphate)

30. What is sludge? (solid waste from sewage treatment plants)

31. What annually uses the most water in homes: dishwashers, toilets, or bathtubs? (toilets)

32. Name three things that can contaminate lakes, streams, rivers, and oceans. (pesticides, fertilizers, trash, human sewage, agricultural waste, industrial chemicals, acid rain, dirt and other sediment, oil and gasoline, and so on)

33. Name a product in your house or garage that can cause water pollution. (cleaners, silver polish, pesticides, paint thinner, motor oil, laundry detergent, and so on)

34. Name four garbage items that can be recycled. (glass bottles, plastic soda bottles, branches and leaves, motor oil, and so on)

35. What does a resource recovery plant do? (sorts trash and recovers the metals, paper, and other valuable materials, and then burns the remaining trash to produce energy)

36. Give three examples of hazardous waste. (pesticides, oil, paint thinner, acids, explosives, radioactive waste, and so on)

37. How do we currently dispose of more than 75 percent of our trash? (by dumping it in landfills)

38. What is *integrated waste managment?* (waste disposal system that makes use of recycling, source reduction, incineration, and landfilling)

39. Name several types of farm waste that contribute to pollution problems. (manure, crop residues, pesticides, fertilizers, and so on)

40. Define *biodegradable*. (having the ability to be broken down into simpler substances by bacteria and other organisms)

41. What are three ways that plastic contributes to global pollution problems? (made from oil, which if spilled during transport can pollute water; manufacturing process creates air pollution; plastic litter can strangle or entangle wildlife; adds to solid waste problem)

42. How does recycling save energy and resources? (eliminates need to extract and process more raw materials, which depletes natural resources and uses more energy)

43. [worth two pollutants] Name three ways cars contribute to air, land, and water pollution. (see page 8)

44. Name three ways people can reduce pollution caused by cars. (carpool, walk, bike, or use public transportation; recycle used motor oil; keep cars tuned up for better fuel efficiency; recycle air-conditioning coolant; and so on)

45. How can dirt and other sediment harm aquatic animals and plants when it washes into lakes, rivers, and streams? (smothers bottom-dwelling organisms; clogs fish gills; keeps sunlight from reaching aquatic plants; decreases visibility, making it harder for some animals to find food; and so on)

46. Explain why biodegradable materials don't break down in landfills. (lack of water and oxygen prevents bacteria and other organisms from breaking down landfill materials)

47. What are three ways that communities can help reduce pollution? (set up recycling programs, provide public transportation, sponsor hazardous waste pickup days, and so on)

48. [worth two pollutants] Name a national law that was passed to help reduce pollution. (see page 83)

49. [worth two pollutants] Give an example of a technology that causes pollution problems *and* an example of a technology that cuts down on pollution problems. (causes problems—cars, power plants, plastic, and so on; solves problems—smokestack scrubbers, catalytic converters, biodegradable plastics, and so on)

50. Name two energy sources that create minimal pollution. (solar, wind, and geothermal power)

51. Name three ways that consumers can help cut pollution. (buy products in recycled and recyclable packaging; buy in bulk; don't buy overpackaged goods, toxic products, and disposable items; write to companies; and so on)

52. Name two ways that acid rain affects the environment. (speeds up the erosion of buildings and statues; can kill some fish and other aquatic animals and can harm their eggs and young; may make trees more susceptible to disease, cold, and insect attack)

USDA—Soil Conservation Service

MARTY SLOVICH, ROVING REPORTER

New York City journalist Marty Slovich knows about pollution. She ought to—she's been following and reporting on important pollution events for over 40 years. *The World News Report*, the magazine Marty works for, sends her out on assignment across the country and around the world. While traveling, Marty keeps a journal to record where she goes and what she learns. Here are some of her journal entries:

Dec. 1952: Finished story in Paris, France, and flew north across English Channel. Saw River Thames as plane circled to land. Sent here to cover story of British "killer fog." Combination of weather conditions trapped blanket of air pollution over capital city for four days this month. Thousands dead!

1. _____ (city)

Dec. 1969: Near Minamata Bay here in the northwest Pacific. Cover-up exposed about mysterious illnesses from mercury poisoning occurring here for past 12 years! Mercury was dumped in the bay by a local factory. It poisoned fish and people who ate the fish. Plan to leave this Asian island nation tomorrow. Will cross the sea and head due west for Korea.

2. _____ (country)

Apr. 22, 1970: Thousands hit streets to demonstrate here and throughout country to protest pollution and other environmental problems. They're calling it "Earth Day." Went down to Fifth Avenue to photograph crowds. Will make great feature story. By the way, it's great to be back in my own house for a change!

3. _____ (city)

Mar. 23, 1980: Flew from home down to the western shore of the Yucatan Peninsula. I'm just south of the Tropic of Cancer on the Bay of Campeche. Doing follow-up story about offshore oil rig. Exploded more than nine months ago—gushed oil 'til it was finally "capped" today. About 600,000 tons spilled into bay waters. Winds kept oil from reaching this coast, but some drifted across Gulf toward Texas. Not sure how much damage to wildlife.

4. _____ (country)

Nov. 1986: On assignment in Rome yesterday when got call about fire at chemical plant near Rhine River. Caught northbound plane and crossed border—flight over Alps was breathtaking! Landed in Bern and took train to factory site. Everything in a 200-mile stretch of the Rhine was killed by chemicals that washed into river from the factory.

5. _____ (country)

Sep. 16, 1987: Took train north yesterday from upstate N.Y. Crossed U.S. border and finally reached Montreal last night. "Montreal Protocol" treaty signed by representatives from more than 20 countries here today. Treaty designed to make substantial cutbacks in use of ozone-depleting CFCs.

6. _____ (country)

Jun. 1988: Down here in sunny U.S. semitropics on the southeast peninsula. Orlando Wilderness Park just opened to the public. Lots of great wildlife here. Especially neat because artificial wetlands were created that naturally treat sewage wastewater from the city. So far, so good—a park for people, habitat for wildlife, solution to water pollution.

7. _____ (state)

May 1988: My first trip to Africa! Doing a story about carbon dioxide (CO_2) pollution and global climate change. Trees help absorb CO_2 from atmosphere, but forest cover in this eastern country reduced from 30 percent to just 1 percent in past four years! More CO_2 and less forest cover may lead to gradual warming of the atmosphere. Hope to get time off to visit wildlife preserve in Kenya. Can catch southbound plane from Addis Ababa.

8. _____ (country)

Jan. 11, 1990: Weather's fantastic here! Great to be south of the equator this winter. Covering international conference on problems of global climate change due to air pollution. Clearing of forest in this country—the largest in South America—may be part of problem. Burning the forest releases tons of CO_2 into air and contributes to greenhouse effect.

9. _____ (country)

1. FOSSIL FUELS

2. AUTO AIR CONDITIONERS

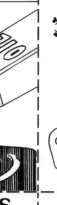

3. CAR CARE

4. JUNKED CARS AND TIRES

5. CAR MANUFACTURING

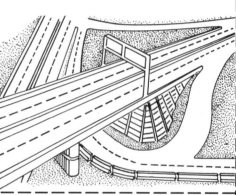

6. ROADS

A. _____

- mining for metals creates waste and causes soil erosion
- making different car parts creates air pollution and waste
- materials left over after assembling and painting cars may be toxic

B. _____

- can leak ozone-destroying CFCs into atmosphere
- can reduce fuel efficiency

C. _____

- building creates waste and causes soil erosion
- construction is an eyesore
- made with asphalt, an oil-based product
- increased traffic creates air and noise pollution
- salt is used in winter to melt snow and ice

D. _____

- drilling and transporting can result in spills
- can leak onto ground and into waterways
- burning creates hazardous exhaust
- pumping releases toxic fumes

E. _____

- are an eyesore
- take up valuable land space
- valuable steel, aluminum, and other resources go to waste
- toxic substances can leak into air or water supplies

F. _____

- cleaning detergents can wash into water supplies
- loose seals can cause oil, anti-freeze, and CFCs to leak
- old parts and used oil and anti-freeze are often dumped illegally
- untuned engines waste fuel
- under-inflated tires reduce fuel efficiency

TRASH AND TOXICS

At present we have more reliable information about Neptune than we do about this country's solid waste stream," says William Rathje, an archaeologist at the University of Arizona. Rathje calls himself a "garbologist" because for the last 20 years he has been digging his way through America's garbage—the bags, bones, books, bottles, and other trash buried deep in landfills. And he's discovering that we have a long way to go before we really understand what happens to the trash we dump every day.

TALKIN' TRASH

Five billion tons. That's the estimated amount of solid waste Americans generate each year. *Solid waste* is whatever we throw away that is in a solid or semi-solid state. About 10-15 percent of it is *hazardous* (see definition below). But all of it can harm people, wildlife, and the environment.

Sifting Through Solid Waste: The five billion tons of solid waste we generate includes agricultural waste (mostly manure and crop leftovers), mining waste (piles of rock, dirt, sand, and slimy mining residue), and industrial waste (scrap metal, plastic, paper, sewage sludge, ash from power plants, and so on). It also includes the waste from homes, schools, hospitals, and businesses, which garbage professionals call *municipal solid waste.*

All of the waste that we throw away becomes part of the nation's *solid waste stream,* which experts say is steadily increasing. Currently, each person alone already adds about four pounds of trash to the solid waste stream every day. And if you total up what we toss, it's easy to see why we've got a solid waste crisis: We throw away enough iron and steel to continuously supply all the nation's automakers; enough aluminum to rebuild our entire commercial airfleet every three months; enough office and writing paper annually to build a wall 12 feet high stretching from Los Angeles to New York City; and enough glass bottles and jars to fill the 1350-foot twin towers of New York's World Trade Center every two weeks.*

Hazardous Nightmares: Hazardous waste doesn't fit neatly into the solid waste definition. This is waste that is flammable, corrosive, unstable, or radioactive, or that contains dangerous substances such as pesticides or lead. Although most of this waste is either itself in a solid or semi-solid state, or stored in barrels or canisters that are considered solid waste, some of it is in a liquid or gaseous state. For example, hazardous waste that pours out of factories and sewers directly into water systems and the hazardous radioactive materials that are produced by the military and by nuclear power plants are not considered part of the solid waste stream. However, both result in significant amounts of waste and create serious pollution problems.

More than 70 percent of hazardous waste is generated by the chemical industry. But small businesses and households also produce an enormous amount each year.

AWAY WITH WASTE

What do we do with all our waste? It varies, depending on the type. Most agricultural waste, for example, is plowed back into the soil. However, some agricultural waste, such as pesticides, fertilizers, and other substances, often ends up

*Source: Environmental Defense Fund

USDA—Soil Conservation Service

washing into water supplies where it can create serious pollution problems. And industrial and municipal solid waste is often dumped in landfills. Here's more about disposal strategies that are currently in use:

Dump It! More than 75 percent of our trash ends up in *landfills*—depressions in the ground that are lined with clay or plastic and then filled with garbage. The garbage is spread out and compacted daily, then covered with a layer of dirt or plastic. Although they create less of a health hazard than open dumps of the past, in which garbage was neither compacted nor covered, landfills have their share of problems. Many—especially those that have been built on wetlands, gravel pits, and other areas with porous soils—are now experiencing problems with *leaching.* Leaching occurs when battery acids, pesticides, and other hazardous waste leak through soils and into surface water and groundwater. Besides problems with leaching, landfills can also be expensive to operate, can create noise and visual pollution, and can cause dangerous levels of explosive methane gas to build up in the layers of compacted garbage.

Garbologists are also discovering that many of the biodegradable materials that we've always asssumed would decompose in a landfill—don't. They've uncovered 50-year-old carrots, steaks, newspapers, hotdogs, and other "biodegradable" items that are still intact. These items haven't decomposed because oxygen, which bacteria and most other decomposers need, doesn't penetrate the compacted layers of a landfill.

Because the amount of trash we produce continues to grow and because much of it doesn't degrade, many of our landfills are filling up. And in many areas, safe sites for new landfills are getting tougher to find (see page 28 for more about landfills).

Burn It! We currently burn about 10 percent of our trash in incinerators, although this percentage is increasing in many parts of the country. But, just as with landfills, there are pros and cons to this "up-in-smoke" method of waste disposal. Incinerators reduce the volume of trash, but they're expensive to build and operate. Incineration also creates air pollution and toxic ash residue. Much of this ash is dumped in landfills or disposed of illegally. And no matter where it's dumped, toxic ash can potentially leach into groundwater (see page 28 for more about incineration).

Recycle or Reuse It! We Americans currently recycle or reuse only about 10 percent of our waste. Although this percentage is starting to grow, our recycling efforts lag behind those of most other industrialized countries. In some areas, local governments encourage recycling by sponsoring curbside pickup of glass, metal, and paper. In other areas, citizens sort their trash and haul it themselves to local recycling centers. And in a few cities, garbage is sorted at *resource recovery plants,* where the reusable and recyclable materials are recovered, and the remaining waste is incinerated to produce energy. But so far most recovery plants have not been cost effective. As a result, many have been forced to close.

In a few areas, composting plants take biodegradable waste such as crop waste, slaughterhouse leftovers, and animal manure, and mix it with soil to create compost. The compost is then bagged and sold as a soil conditioner and fertilizer. Unfortunately, there's still not much demand for compost in the U.S.

Bury or Inject It! Disposing of acids, pesticides, dioxins, toxic ash, radioactive waste, sewage sludge, and other types of hazardous waste has become our nation's most dangerous waste problem. Most hazardous waste is dumped in landfills or incinerated, which, as we already mentioned, creates toxic runoff and air pollution. But much has also been buried deep underground or injected into cracks and crevices of underground rock layers. Due to inappropriate storage, many of these underground hazardous materials are leaking into surrounding soils and groundwater, creating serious cleanup problems. The EPA has already identified thousands of hazardous waste sites that pose a threat to people, wildlife, and the environment. Despite the fact that laws regulating hazardous waste disposal are tougher than ever before, many hazardous materials are still disposed of illegally. And for many hazardous wastes, such as radioactive waste, there are no completely safe disposal methods.

SOLID WASTE SOLUTIONS

Most experts would agree there's no simple solution to our waste woes. But striving to reduce the overall amount of waste we produce is the first step. *Source reduction* not only reduces waste, it also saves money and conserves resources and raw materials. Source reduction means designing products that last longer and use less packaging. It means producing and using fewer hazardous products. It means buying only what you need and selectively buying the most environmentally sound products. And it means throwing away the "throwaway" mentality.

But even with an increased focus on producing less, we'll always have waste. And many experts agree that an *integrated waste management* approach is best—one that focuses on source reduction in addition to recycling and safe incineration and landfilling.

Let's Hear It for Recycling: Reusing and recycling what we've traditionally tossed makes economic and environmental sense. By not burning or dumping as much waste as they have in the past, communities and businesses are saving money and conserving resources.

Although most people are behind recycling efforts, some environmentalists are worried that some recycling programs may discourage source reduction and encourage the use of environmentally damaging products. For example, many environmentalists do not support certain plastic recycling efforts because they feel it encourages plastic use. They feel that the benefits of recycling do not justify producing more plastic in the first place because plastic manufacturing uses fossil fuels and creates toxic by-products. On the other hand, some environmentalists support plastic recycling research because they feel that plastic products are here to stay and plastic recycling will save landfill space, eliminate plastic incineration, and encourage the recycling habit.

High-Tech Solutions: Well-designed and safely sited landfills, efficient resource recovery plants, and other high-tech but environmentally sound operations should also be a part of the solution to our waste problems. But even though new discoveries can help design safer landfills and recovery plants, many environmentalists caution people against counting on technology to solve all our waste woes. Often technological "fixes" don't work as planned and can create new environmental hazards that are more damaging than the problems they were meant to solve.

The Secret of Success: A successful integrated waste management program has one more key component—education. An educated public knows what happens to its waste. An educated public keeps abreast of innovative laws that encourage recycling, such as bottle bills and packaging taxes. An educated public is on the lookout for advertising scams like those that try to sell "degradable" plastics that don't really degrade. And above all, an educated public realizes that as far as waste goes, "less is definitely best!"

Trash Can-Do

Learn about the composition of household trash, and then sing a song while showing how to reduce, reuse, and recycle.

Objectives:
Discuss different kinds of household trash. Describe three ways to cut down on trash.

Ages:
Primary

Materials:
- *posterboard*
- *chalkboard or easel paper*
- *index cards*
- *crayons or markers*
- *tape*
- *magazines (optional)*
- *scissors (optional)*
- *glue (optional)*

Subjects:
Social Studies, Language Arts, Math, and Music

Anybody who takes out trash knows how fast it can pile up. In this activity, your kids can find out what's typically found in household trash, and then think of ways to reduce the amount of trash they produce.

Before getting started, copy the diagram below onto a large piece of posterboard. Mark off the different sections on the trash can as shown in the diagram. (These dimensions will work for a group of about 25 kids.) Put the trash can drawing where everyone can see and easily reach it. Also copy the phrase "Reduce, Reuse, Recycle" on a piece of paper and tape it near the can. Finally, copy each of the trash items printed in **bold** type under "Trash or Treasure?" on page 19 onto a separate index card. (We've included items for 25 children.)

PART 1: TALKIN' TRASH

Begin by having the kids think about the trash their families throw out every day. Ask for examples of things the kids might find in their trash at home and list the items on a chalkboard or sheet of easel paper. Then point out the diagram you copied earlier and tell the kids that the trash can is marked to show the different kinds of materials found in trash: paper products, food waste, yard waste, glass, metal, and plastic. "Other" includes all the stuff that doesn't neatly fit into any of the above categories, such as bike tires, old furniture, wood, rubber, cloth, toys made with a combination of materials, and so on.

Go back to the list of trash items the kids came up with earlier and have the kids decide which category on the diagram each item would fit into. For example, leftovers and orange rinds would be food waste, raked leaves and weeds would be yard waste, old magazines and cardboard boxes would be paper products, empty dog food cans and foil would be metal, and so on.

Next tell the kids that they're going to draw some pictures of things their families might throw away, and then they'll fill up the trash can diagram with their "trash." Pass out crayons or markers and give each child one of the trash item index cards you made earlier. Help each child read the trash item written on his or her card, and then have the child draw the item on the back of the card. (Or you could have the kids look for pictures of their items in magazines, cut out the pictures, and glue them onto their cards.)

After the kids have drawn their pictures, ask if anyone has an item made from paper or cardboard. Have those kids come up to the trash can diagram and tape their cards to the paper section. Continue with the other materials, having the kids take turns "throwing away their trash" by coming up and attaching their cards to the appropriate sections.

PART 2: LIGHTEN THE LOAD

Use the background information on pages 14-16 to explain how trash can lead to problems, such as litter, overflowing landfills, toxic pollution, and wasted resources. Then ask the kids if they can think of any solutions to the problems caused by too much trash. Tell them that one way is to make less trash in the first place. See if they can come up with some ways to create less trash. Then use the information under "Remember the 3 Rs" on page 18 to explain the three words that can help remind people how to make less trash: reduce, reuse, and recycle.

Now tell the kids it's time to see if they can reduce, reuse, or recycle the things they just put "into the trash." Explain that each child should think of one way to keep from throwing away the item on his or her card. Have the kids take turns coming up to the diagram. They should remove their cards, state what they can do with the items instead of throwing them away or how they can avoid having them in the first place, and then tape the cards under the "3 Rs" sign you put up earlier. Use the information under "Trash or Treasure?" to help discuss

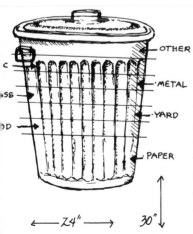

OTHER
METAL
YARD
PAPER

← 24" → 30"

each child's options. Ideas will vary depending on the solutions the children choose. For example, we've suggested recycling as an option for materials that may be collected through local recycling programs. But if your community doesn't have a program in place or doesn't recycle a particular material, the kids may think of one of the other solutions we've included or may come up with other ideas of their own. (*Note:* You may want to contact your local department of solid waste or recycling to find out what materials can be recycled in your community.)

As each child completes his or her turn, have the group sing the "Trash in the Can" song at the right. Begin the song with the number of kids in your group and count down with each verse until you have 0

pieces of trash in the can.

Ask the kids if they think it's possible to reduce, reuse, or recycle *everything* in their trash at home as they did in this activity. (No. There will always be some materials that must be discarded, depending on what they are and on what local recycling programs can accommodate.)

TRASH IN THE CAN

(Sing to the tune of "99 Bottles of Beer on the Wall.")
25 pieces of trash in the can,
25 pieces of trash.
Take one out,
And then you can shout:
24 pieces of trash in the can!

ACTION TIP!

BUILD A TRASH MENAGERIE

Make cardboard or wooden boxes for recyclable or reusable items, and decorate the boxes to look like different animals. You might make a box to keep scrap paper in or boxes to hold materials you plan to recycle, such as glass bottles, aluminum cans, or paper. You could also make a swap-box for things the kids don't want anymore but that someone else might want.

REMEMBER THE 3 RS

Practicing the following tips not only cuts down on the amount of trash people generate, but also saves resources and energy:
REDUCE trash by not buying overpackaged products, disposable products, or products that you don't really need. Also repair broken objects or mend torn clothes instead of throwing them out.
REUSE whatever you can, such as the backs of paper for scratch paper, empty containers for storage, and old cloth for

cleaning rags. And you can give away clothes you outgrow, books you've read, and toys you no longer want so someone else can use them.
RECYCLE whatever you can. For example, many communities collect glass, aluminum, newspaper, and some plastics to make into new products. You can also recycle food scraps and yard clippings by making a compost pile.

Tim Farnham

TRASH OR TREASURE?

PAPER
newspaper: *recycle; reuse* for lining pet cages, covering the floor when painting, and so on
magazine: *recycle; reuse* by sharing with a friend, taking to a doctor's office, or cutting out pictures
notebook paper: *recycle; reuse* (use both sides)
paper towel: *reduce* by using cloth towel or napkin, or a sponge
paper plate: *reduce* by using reusable plates
individual-serving cereal box: *reduce* by buying cereal in large boxes or in bulk
paper napkin: *reduce* by using a cloth napkin

FOOD AND YARD WASTE
apple core, banana peel, burned toast, dead flowers, leaves: *recycle* by composting

METAL
aluminum soda can: *recycle*
aluminum foil: *recycle; reduce* by storing leftover food in reusable containers
bent coat hanger: *reuse* by making a mobile or other craft with it

GLASS
empty orange juice bottle: *recycle; reuse* for storing other liquids
empty glass soda bottle: *recycle*
empty mayonnaise jar: *recycle; reuse* for storage

PLASTIC
plastic foam cup: *recycle; reduce* by using reusable cups

plastic grocery bag: *recycle; reuse* for shopping or storage; *reduce* by shopping with your own reusable bag
disposable pen: *reduce* by using refillable pen
empty yogurt container: *reuse* for storage; *reduce* by making your own yogurt or buying in larger containers

OTHER
torn shirt: *reduce* by mending; *reuse* as a rag
broken bike: *reduce* by fixing
old checkers game: *reuse* by giving to someone else

In the Dumps

Do a demonstration and answer questions about decomposition.

Objectives:
Define decomposition, biodegradable, landfill, and compost. Describe decomposition.

Ages:
Intermediate

Materials:
* *small plastic containers (about 16 oz.) with lids*
* *trowel or spoon*
* *soil*
* *newspaper*
* *"trash" materials (see activity)*
* *water*
* *spray bottle (optional)*

Subjects:
Science and Social Studies

By setting up a demonstration and monitoring it for several weeks, your group can make some discoveries about the garbage that ends up in landfills.

Start the activity by explaining that *decomposition* is the process by which materials break down. For example, air, water, sunlight, and other agents break down inorganic, or nonliving, materials such as rocks and metals. But living organisms break down organic materials such as food waste, wood, and dead animals—materials that come directly or indirectly from other living things. Because they're broken down by living organisms, these materials are said to be *biodegradable*. (Just about anything is *degradable* and will eventually break down, given the proper conditions and enough time.)

When an organism dies, it is broken down by a succession of other living things. Initially scavengers, such as vultures or beetles, feed on the dead organism. Later *decomposers* such as bacteria and fungi, including yeasts and molds, break down the material even further. As these microorganisms consume the organic material, they produce waste products that serve as nutrients for plants and other living things. This is a very efficient process of disposing of waste—all the materials are recycled. (Warm, moist, and well-aerated conditions are ideal for most decomposers. Certain organisms can biodegrade organic material in the absence of oxygen, but the process is very slow.) Now have the kids try the following demonstration to see how different types of trash decompose under different conditions.

(continued next page)

USDA—Soil Conservation Service

SETTING UP THE DEMONSTRATION

Divide the group into small teams. Give each team two plastic containers with lids and have the kids label one container "A" and the other "B." (The containers should also be identified according to team.)

Next provide—or have the kids bring in—enough of the following "trash" materials so each team will have two small samples of each: paper towel, aluminum foil, wax paper, plastic wrap, plastic foam, cracker, leaf.

Take the group outside to dig up some soil for their containers. Choose a place that is likely to contain microorganisms, such as under a tree or shrub. But be sure that the kids take no more soil than they'll need to fill their containers and that they disturb the area as little as possible.

When they're back inside, have each team set up their containers as follows:

1. Fill each container about halfway with soil.

2. Place a piece of each "trash" item on top of the soil. Use items of the same type and size for each container.

3. Cover the items by filling up the containers with more soil.

4. Put a lid on container A and set the container aside. Spray the contents of container B with water until the soil is thoroughly moistened but not soggy. Leave container B open and set it next to container A. (At the end of each day or so, spray the contents of container B with a little water, and then put on the lid and shake the container to allow air and moisture to get between the soil particles and around the items. Keep the lid on overnight to reduce evaporation, but remove it in the morning and leave the container open during the day.)

Also have each team make a chart, which they'll use to describe what happens in their containers (see example). Then ask the teams to make these predictions: Will all the items in each container show signs of breaking down? If not, which won't? Will some items break down more quickly than others? If so, in what order will they break down? Will the items in one container break down more quickly than those in the other? If so, in which container?

SAMPLE CHART

	CRACKER		LEAF		PAPER TOWEL		WAX PAPER	
	A	B	A	B	A	B	A	B
Week 1								
Week 2								
Week 3								

CHECKING THE PREDICTIONS

At the end of the first week, have the teams follow this procedure:

1. Empty the contents of each container onto a separate sheet of newspaper.

2. Look for each of the trash items and separate them from the soil.

3. Fill in the chart for Week 1 by describing any decomposition that took place during the week in each of the items from each container. For any item that showed no signs of breaking down, write "no change" in the appropriate space.

4. Put half the soil from container A back into its container, put the container A items

back inside, cover them with the remaining container A soil, and replace the lid. Repeat for container B, but continue to keep the contents moist and to leave the lid off during the day.

5. Continue this process once a week for at least four weeks.

At the end of the four-week period, have the kids analyze their data and discuss how accurate their predictions were. Also have the different teams share their data. Use the questions on the next page to discuss what happened in the demonstration. Afterward tell the kids that the materials that decomposed were biodegradable and those that didn't decompose were nonbiodegradable.

- Which items showed signs of decomposition? (cracker, leaf, paper towel, wax paper) Which items, if any, decomposed completely? (answers may vary) Which showed no signs of decomposition? (foil, plastic wrap, plastic foam)
- In which container did the items decompose the most? (B)
- What conditions were the same for both containers? (They had the same kind of soil and trash items.) What conditions were different? (The contents of container B were shaken and exposed to more air and water.)
- Were there any differences between your team's results and those of the other teams? If so, how could you explain them? (Other teams may have used different-sized items or different amounts of moisture, or their soil samples may have had more or fewer microorganisms.)

LOADED-UP LANDFILLS

After your discussion, explain to the group that most garbage currently is dumped in *landfills*. Use the background information on page 15 to explain what a landfill is. Also describe some of the problems with landfills, such as why materials—even organic waste—break down so slowly in landfills. Then explain that *composting* is an alternative method of disposing of organic waste. Unlike garbage in a landfill, composted waste is kept moist and well aerated, and is not compacted.

USDA—Soil Conservation Service

Now have the kids apply what they've learned about decomposition and landfills to answer the following questions:

- Which container in the demonstration approximates conditions in a landfill? (A) In a compost pile? (B) Explain your answers. (Materials in container A were closed off from the air; materials in container B were kept moist and aerated.)
- What might explain any decomposition that occurred in container A? (The soil and items in container A had a small amount of air and moisture; the soil also may have had microorganisms that don't require oxygen.)
- There's more paper in landfills than any other material—about 38 percent by volume. Also, about 15 percent of the material by volume is food and yard waste and about 34 percent is metal, glass, and plastic. Based on these facts and what you know about landfills, why would you say landfills are not the best way to dispose of most of our garbage? (Even though most of the material that ends up in landfills is biodegradable, there's not enough air and moisture to help break it down. Also, the metal and glass that could be recycled and the organic materials that could be composted and reused are wasted.) What can individuals do to avoid sending so much garbage to landfills? (reduce the amount of garbage they generate, recycle organic waste by composting it, recycle or reuse consumer products whenever possible)

Note: To examine decomposition in action, you might want to take the kids outside and have them investigate a decaying log. (See "A Rottin' Place to Live" on page 41 of *NatureScope—Trees Are Terrific!*)

Garbage Shuffle

Discuss trash disposal through history and perform a trash rap.

Objectives:
Describe how people have disposed of solid waste through history. Describe several problems related to solid waste disposal.

Ages:
Intermediate and Advanced

Materials:
• *copies of page 29*
• *materials to make costumes and props (optional)*

Subjects:
History, Social Studies, and Music

I f you were an archaeologist, you could sift through the dusty remains of every human population since prehistoric times and discover something common to all of them: trash. By performing a trash rap, the kids in your group can learn about the history of how people have dealt with trash.

Begin by asking the group how people get rid of their trash. (by dumping it, burying it, or burning it) Explain that the task of getting rid of garbage has been around as long as people have existed. Next pass out copies of page 29 and have the kids read through the rap. Then use the information under "A History of Trash" on the next page to discuss the disposal method common to the time period depicted in each of the verses. Use these questions during your discussion:

• What kinds of trash have people thrown out during different periods? How did they dispose of it?
• Why could prehistoric hunters throw trash on the ground without any problems? How did trash cause problems in ancient Rome, medieval London, and 19th-century U.S. cities?
• What kinds of pollution can trash create?
• What are some problems with dumping trash at sea that aren't mentioned in the rap?
• Some people think we should launch our trash into outer space. What do you think about this idea?

DO THE TRASH RAP

Now tell the kids that they can perform the rap. Have a volunteer who can demonstrate the rap rhythm read the first verse out loud so the group can get an idea of how the rap will sound. Then assign each of the verses in the rap to a different child or small group of kids. Everybody can join in for the chorus.

Be sure to give the kids plenty of time to practice their verses. And have them coordinate some moves to accompany the chorus, such as shuffling from side to side and clapping. Encourage them to make up appropriate actions for the verses too, such as pointing their fingers or shaking their heads. You could also have the group make costumes and props to fit the different rap roles. The kids may want to perform the rap for other groups to teach them about how people have disposed of trash through time.

When the kids are ready to perform, have them stand in a semicircle. Start out with everyone doing the chorus, while the first "soloist" or small group moves out in front to do the first verse. At the end of the first verse, repeat the chorus while the first performer(s) returns to the semicircle and the second performer(s) steps up front. Continue alternating the verses with the chorus until the end of the rap.

Afterward you can have the kids create a trash time line, using drawings and short summaries to describe the various periods depicted in the rap. You might also want to have the group make up a new rap verse to describe the kinds of trash people might generate in the future and the ways they might dispose of it.

Activity idea adapted from "The Throwaway Three," written by Fay Bradley and published in *A-Way with Waste*, a curriculum guide published by the Washington State Department of Ecology.

Luise Woelflein

1. Africa, 1.5 million years ago

Many prehistoric hunter-gatherers simply threw trash on the ground around their camps. Others sometimes had special places to dump their refuse. Made mostly of biodegradable items, the trash generally decomposed. Even nonbiodegradable objects, such as old stone tools, never accumulated to any significant amount because people lived in small groups and moved from place to place.

2. Ancient Greece, 500 BC

For a time, city residents in ancient Greece and Rome threw their trash out into the streets. Human scavengers regularly picked through the waste for reusable items, a practice which continues even today in many parts of the world. Road levels grew higher and higher from the onslaught of trash. Old, torn-down homes were used as foundations to make newly built homes level with the roads. People in Greece finally organized a system of municipal trash collection, carrying waste to dumps at least a mile outside of town.

3. Medieval London, AD 1350

People in the Middle Ages threw trash, food, and human waste out into the streets, where it caused a problem in densely populated cities such as London. The mess contributed to the spread of various diseases. (The bubonic plague was one disease that became epidemic. It was spread by fleas from infected rats, which swarmed through crowded cities.)

4. Atlantic Ocean, AD 1500

People throughout most of history have considered the ocean limitless and have dumped trash into it without hesitation. The trash and food waste dumped during the age of ocean exploration usually disintegrated in the salt water. But today, the plastic, sewage, hazardous waste, and other materials we dump are harming marine life and washing up onto beaches, where they can be dangerous to people and coastal wildlife. It's estimated that people around the world dump nearly 14 billion pounds of waste into oceans each year.

5. New York City, 1860

During the Industrial Revolution, large industrial cities in the U.S. became filthier than other cities in previous periods. Dead horses, coal and wood ash from furnaces, and kitchen and animal waste filled streets and alleys. Pigs roamed the streets, eating much of the food waste. Rats and roaches also invaded the rotting mess, and there were epidemics of disease. For a time, people believed that the foul fumes carried germs that could be transmitted to people. Although this theory was disproved around 1880, the concern about public health did lead to city street cleaning and better-regulated municipal collection and disposal.

6. United States, 1920

Open dumps have been around since prehistoric times and remained a common method of disposal in the U.S. until after World War II, when landfills became the favored method. Long before that time, though, people complained about problems associated with open dumps, such as rodents, fires, and odors.

7. Los Angeles, 1930

The large-scale burning of trash in incineration plants had been used on and off as a waste-disposal method since the 1870s. Although incinerators significantly reduced the volume of trash, citizens complained about the smoke and odors from these plants. Many of the incinerators that were common in hundreds of U.S. cities during the 1930s were later closed down.

8. United States, 1960

The period after World War II marked the rise of the throwaway lifestyle and use of synthetic materials. Households no longer burned much wood or coal, but they generated more waste from disposable products and packaging materials, including a lot of paper and plastic trash. They also began throwing out more toxic substances that ended up in dumps and landfills. These hazardous materials leached through the soil into water supplies. And when dumps caught fire and smoldered, toxic fumes were released into the air. It later became clear that, as landfills filled up, siting new, "safe" ones would become more and more difficult.

9. United States, 1973

A movement to control the increasing volume of garbage going into landfills led to a revival of interest in incineration. New technology focused on converting waste to energy through incineration. Incinerators became known as "resource recovery" plants, such as the one described in the rap. Not only do these plants reduce the volume of trash, they also produce usable energy. This was seen as an added benefit after an oil crisis raised concern about the nation's limited energy sources. But the plants emit noxious fumes, are expensive to build and run, and produce a highly toxic ash. Because of these problems, these plants have yet to gain widespread acceptance.

10. United States, 1990

Citizens in the U.S. and throughout the world have begun to reduce, reuse, and recycle to cut down on the total amount of materials entering the solid waste stream and to save natural resources.

Tons of Trash

Use some statistics to answer questions about municipal solid waste, and then conduct a survey and discuss solid waste scenarios.

Objectives:
Define solid waste. Interpret and graph data to answer questions about solid waste. Design and conduct a solid waste survey. Discuss attitudes relating to solid waste issues.

Ages:
Advanced

Materials:
- *copies of pages 30 and 31*
- *graph paper*
- *rulers*
- *colored pencils or markers*
- *calculators (optional)*

Subjects:
Social Studies and Math

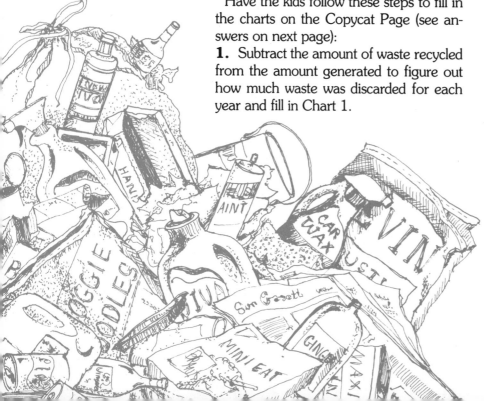

The world has a growing garbage crisis—and all of us contribute to it. In the first part of this activity, your group will find out more about the problem by working with some solid waste statistics. In the second part, they'll get a chance to survey others and explore their own attitudes about solid waste issues.

PART 1: WASTE A-WEIGH

Use the background information on page 14 to explain solid waste and the solid waste stream to the kids. Then tell your group that they'll learn about some trends concerning the trash people toss from homes and businesses. This trash, collected and disposed of by the city or community, is called *municipal solid waste.* Begin by passing out copies of page 30 and telling the kids that they'll be completing the charts on that page to find out more about municipal solid waste in the U.S. between 1960 and 1985. Then they can use the information in the charts to draw some graphs and answer the questions on the page. (If the kids won't be using calculators, you may want to have them round the statistics in the charts to the nearest whole number before doing the problems.)

Have the kids follow these steps to fill in the charts on the Copycat Page (see answers on next page):

1. Subtract the amount of waste recycled from the amount generated to figure out how much waste was discarded for each year and fill in Chart 1.

2. Find the average number of pounds of trash each person generated per day for each year and fill in Chart 3. (weight *generated* each year [Chart 1] divided by population in the same year [Chart 2] multiplied by 2000 pounds per ton, divided by 365 days per year)

3. Find the *weight* of each discarded material for 1960 and 1985 and fill in Chart 5. (total amount *discarded* per year [Chart 1] multiplied by percentage of each material in the same year [Chart 4]) *Note:* Chart 4 shows the composition of the total waste *after* recyclable materials were removed. "Other" includes materials such as wood, cloth, rubber, leather, and so on. The percentages may not add up to exactly 100 percent because of rounding off.

Next pass out graph paper, a ruler, and some colored pencils or markers to each child. Then have the kids follow these steps to draw the graphs shown on the next page:

1. Draw a line graph (A) to show the changes in the total amount of muncipal solid waste generated from 1960 to 1985 (Chart 1).

2. Draw a line graph (B) to show changes in U.S. population from 1960 to 1985 (Chart 2).

3. Draw a comparative bar graph (C) that illustrates the changes in *percentage* of each material in the municipal solid waste stream from 1960 to 1985, using the information in Chart 4 for paper, food and yard waste, metal, glass, and plastic.

Finally, have the kids use their charts and graphs to answer the questions on the Copycat Page. (See answers on the next page.)

Now have your kids think about how they contribute to solid waste problems and how they'd react in various situations. Start by dividing the group into teams of four or five and have each team design a questionnaire to find out what people in their community are doing to help solve solid and hazardous waste problems. Here are some examples of questions they might ask:

- Do you recycle glass? Paper? Aluminum?
- When you go shopping, do you ask for a paper bag, a plastic bag, or do you take your own reusable bag?
- Have you ever taken leftover toxic household materials to a hazardous waste collection site?
- What do you feel is your community's most serious waste disposal problem?

Give the kids some time to conduct their surveys. Then have each team tally up their results and calculate the percentages of different responses for each question. Have the teams report back to the rest of the group, and then have them compare their results.

As a follow-up, pass out copies of page 31 and have the teams discuss the situations on the page. Tell the kids to think about how they might respond in each situation, but explain that there are no right or wrong answers. Also be sure to emphasize that the kids should try to be as honest as possible. Finally point out that, when thinking about how they'd react to the different scenarios, the kids should consider what alternatives may be available, what compromises or sacrifices they may be willing to make, and what effect their actions may have on other people. Have the kids write down their responses, and then discuss what they came up with when everyone's finished.

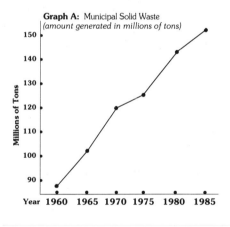

Graph A: Municipal Solid Waste *(amount generated in millions of tons)*

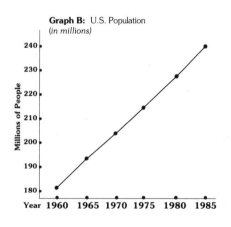

Graph B: U.S. Population *(in millions)*

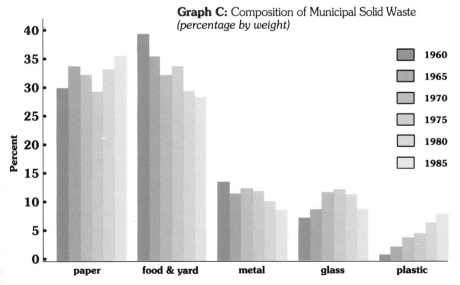

Graph C: Composition of Municipal Solid Waste *(percentage by weight)*

1960
1965
1970
1975
1980
1985

paper   food & yard   metal   glass   plastic

ANSWERS TO SHEET 1
Chart 1: 81.7, 96.1, 112.5, 116.2, 129.2, 137.2
Chart 3: 2.7, 2.9, 3.2, 3.2, 3.4, 3.5
Chart 5: 24.5, 48.7 (paper); 32.2, 40.3 (food & yard); 10.5, 12.3 (metal); 6.4, 12.2 (glass); 0.4, 9.7 (plastic)

1. 6.6%. 10%. 38.1 million tons.
2. Paper and glass. Plastic. More products being made from plastic, especially disposable items.
3. You'd expect it to increase, as long as the amount each person in the community generated didn't decrease substantially. Yes. Increased. More throwaway products, more packaging. (Increased weight in individual items could have contributed, but in general this weight has decreased.)
4. Paper, food and yard waste. Plastic. Food and yard waste, metal. Significant increase of paper, food and yard waste, and plastic being thrown away without a corresponding increase in metal and glass; more products being made with plastic that were once made with heavier metal or glass; increased metal and glass recycling.
5. By volume. By knowing what takes up the most space in landfills, experts can better recommend how to control waste to slow the rate at which landfills fill up. (In 1986 the percentage of plastic in U.S. landfills was only about 7% by weight but 18% by volume. And glass was about 8% by weight but only 2% by volume. Paper made up the greatest percentage of waste, both by weight at about 36% and by volume at 38%.)

Debate several issues relating to solid waste and hazardous substances.

Objectives:
Identify the environmental pros and cons of several consumer issues. List the steps involved in making an environmentally sound decision.

Ages:
Advanced

Materials:
• *easel paper or chalkboard*
• *research materials*

Subjects:
Language Arts, Science, and Social Studies

 aking environmentally sound choices isn't easy. For example, which is better for the environment: paper bags or plastic bags? Cloth diapers or disposables? Many of the choices involve complicated issues that aren't very well understood, and the overall benefits of one choice over those of another aren't always clear. Even when all the facts are in, the decisions we make usually involve some tough trade-offs.

Have your kids research and debate several complex issues to identify the pros and cons of different options and to discuss the trade-offs involved with solid waste decisions. Then, as a group, the kids can come up with a checklist for making an environmentally sound decision.

GETTING READY

Divide the group into discussion teams and assign each team one of the questions listed under "The Issues" on page 28. Explain that each team will be staging a debate on their topic. For example, one team will focus on the issue of whether to choose paper or plastic bags at the grocery store. Some team members will support the use of plastic bags and the others will support the use of paper bags.

Tell team members to read their question and then decide which point of view they want to support. (If individuals have a tough time choosing sides, you can have the team members draw lots to make it fair.) Explain that some team members might end up supporting a position that is different from the one they currently support. Point out that, no matter which side they end up on, they will learn how to develop and support arguments defending a specific point of view, and they will expand their understanding of the issues.

Explain that when the debates take place both sides will have a chance to present their case and rebut what the other team members say. Also mention that everyone on a team should take an active role in the debate.

To prepare for the debate, have team members research their topics, using current periodicals, newspaper articles, and books. Explain that they need to gather information that will help them understand the pros and cons of each alternative and gauge whether or not one alternative is better than another. They will also need to gather facts that support their arguments. (We've listed some of the pros and cons for each debate topic on page 28 to help you

guide the kids' research. Also see "Current Thinking" on the next page to find out what different experts think is the most correct action to take with each issue.)

Before starting, set a time limit for each debate and go over the "Debate Pointers" on the next page. You might also want to set up a debate format, such as:
1. first group presents its case
2. second group presents its case
3. first group rebuts and adds arguments
4. second group rebuts and adds arguments

Explain that the observers have an important role during the debates. They should think about the following questions as they listen to each debate:
• Were the arguments convincing? Do you think the information used to support the case was reliable? Why or why not? (Try to remember specific examples.)
• Were any important issues not addressed?
• Do you feel that one option is better for the environment than another? Why or why not?
• Do you feel that you need additional information before you can decide which position you support? If so, what information would you need?
• Which team was most persuasive and why?

After each debate, have the observers comment on the points they were instructed to keep in mind. Then ask the debaters for their reactions to the debate. Also ask the group to think about other options that were not presented (see "Current Thinking" at the right). For example, in the first debate, the best option for the environment—people bringing a reusable cloth bag to the grocery store—wasn't part of the discussion. Point out that articles and news programs also sometimes leave out important options. Explain that being a responsible citizen means finding out about and understanding all the choices.

Also point out that there's usually not one right or wrong answer and that environmental decisions often involve trade-offs. For example, taxing lawn-care companies that use toxic chemicals could cause some businesses to go bankrupt and some people to lose their jobs. But it could also lower the threat of death and sickness from toxic chemicals.

After all the teams have presented their debates, discuss the issue of solid waste disposal in general, using the background information on pages 14-16. Mention that a combination of methods is important—there's no single right way. Also bring up the point that experts often don't agree on

what the best option is, and that means individuals have to make decisions using the facts and information they have and their own value systems.

As a wrap-up, have the group come up with a short checklist for making an environmentally sound choice. For example, the list might include the following:

- Find out as much information as you can about the different options from reliable sources, including experts in the field.
- Decide who would benefit and who would be harmed by each of the options. (Think about both short- and long-term consequences.)
- Learn how each option would affect the environment and other people around the world.
- Make a list of the pros and cons for each option.
- Weigh the pros and cons to make your choice.

CURRENT THINKING

It's important for kids to realize that because there's so much we don't understand about environmental problems, experts don't always have all the answers. Many solid waste issues don't have clear solutions at this time, and experts feel that more information is needed before they can determine what the best solutions are. Overall, environmentalists support an integrated waste management program that emphasizes source reduction and recycling first, followed by incineration and landfilling. (*Note:* The pros and cons on page 28 are only a partial listing. Each issue is very complex and involves many economic and social issues that we didn't have space to list.)

Issue #1: Environmentalists recommend that shoppers bring a reusable cloth bag to the store instead of getting new paper or plastic bags each time. Some experts say paper and plastic are equally harmful and that if you use either, you should make sure to reuse them. Others always choose paper bags over plastic.

Issue #2: Many environmentalists and public health professionals feel the pros of cloth outweigh the pros of disposables. Others feel that we do not know enough

about the environmental effects throughout the "life cycle" of either to know which is best in the long run.

Issue #3: Most environmentalists aren't in favor of most types of plastic packaging, including plastic soda bottles. The current recommended action is to choose glass over plastic and to recycle the glass. Many environmentalists, however, feel that, although plastic has its problems, it is here to stay, and therefore plastic recycling efforts are important.

Issue #4: Many environmentalists feel that we need to recycle as much as 65 percent of our garbage to handle our solid waste problems and that putting a freeze on building new incinerators and landfills would help promote the reduction, reuse, and recycling of solid waste.

Some people argue that well-managed landfills are more ecologically sound than incinerators. Others say incinerators and landfills are equally bad, though they acknowledge that both will continue to play an important role in solid waste disposal.

Issue #5: Environmentalists favor organic lawn care and encourage landscaping with native plants to attract wildlife and save water.

ISSUE #1:
BAG IT!

Question: If given an option, should you choose a paper or plastic bag for your groceries?

paper bags
pros: made from a renewable resource; biodegradable; recyclable; reusable
cons: most made, at least partially, with virgin fiber instead of recycled paper; timber often grown using chemical fertilizers; paper manufacturing releases toxics and other pollutants into the air and water; bulky; paper takes up more space in landfills than plastic

plastic bags
pros: easier to carry; cheaper to manufacture; leakproof; take up less landfill space; recyclable in some places; reusable; some are made with petroleum waste products
cons: can harm wildlife; most recyclable ones are not recycled; bits of plastic can leach into water supplies as degradable plastic breaks down; most plastics are made from a nonrenewable resource; manufacturing releases toxics and other pollutants into the air and water

ISSUE #2:
THE BABY-BOTTOM COVERUP

Question: Should people buy cloth diapers or disposable diapers?

cloth diapers
pros: often cheaper; reusable; made from renewable resources; biodegradable; human waste treated in sewage treatment plants instead of going into landfills; save landfill space; can prevent rashes in some babies
cons: require energy to manufacture, wash, and deliver; energy-use creates air and water pollution; detergents can create water pollution; cotton often grown using pesticides and chemical fertilizers

disposable diapers
pros: convenient; keep baby's skin drier
cons: human waste can carry disease, creating risk for garbage handlers; made from a nonrenewable resource; nonbiodegradable; manufacturing creates air and water pollution; take up landfill space; degradable ones can break down into tiny bits of plastic that leach into water supplies

ISSUE #3:
SODA SENSE

Question: Should you buy sodas in plastic or glass bottles?

plastic bottles
pros: cheap; lightweight, unbreakable; recyclable in some places; inert in landfills
cons: made from a nonrenewable resource; nonbiodegradable; manufacturing creates air and water pollution; degradables can create water pollution; limited uses for recycled plastic; difficult to sort and recycle; recycled plastic not as durable as virgin plastic

glass bottles
pros: cheaper and easier to recycle; can be recycled many times without losing strength; made from abundant natural resources
cons: heavy; breakable; nonbiodegradable; cost more to transport; recycling uses a lot of water and can create water pollution

ISSUE #4:
BURN, BABY, BURN!

Question: Which is the better alternative for disposing of the solid waste we don't recycle: burning it in incinerators or dumping it in landfills?

incinerators
pros: greatly reduce the volume of trash; save landfill space; can recover energy and resources; reduce the threat of rat, roach, and other pest infestation
cons: expensive to build and operate; may discourage people from recycling (need a high volume of garbage to operate); create toxic ash that can leach into water supplies when landfilled; people don't want them nearby; require separation of trash into burnables and nonburnables

landfills
pros: easy because waste doesn't need to be separated or sorted; generate methane gas, which can be recovered for fuel; can sometimes reuse site for other purposes
cons: hazardous materials can leach into water supplies; generate methane gas, which can cause explosions if not vented; take up valuable land space; buried biodegradable materials don't biodegrade; buried resources are wasted; people don't want them nearby

ISSUE #5:
A "GROWING" DILEMMA

Question: Should homeowners use chemical lawn service companies or rely on organic lawn care? *Note:* Organic lawn care uses no toxic herbicides and pesticides and no chemical fertilizers. People can either take care of their lawns themselves, using organic methods, or hire organic landscaping services.

chemical lawn care
pros: effective in short term for controlling pests; provides "manicured" look; easy
cons: expensive; long-term effects not clear; chemicals made from nonrenewable resources; chemicals wash off in rain and pollute water supplies; chemicals can build up in soil; chemicals can poison people, pets, and wildlife; manufacturing and transporting chemicals can create air and water pollution

organic lawn care
pros: nontoxic; can be less expensive; maintains ecological life-support systems; causes less pollution
cons: can take hard work if professionals not hired; short-term pest control may not be effective

Chorus

Do the garbage shuffle; it's an age-old thrill—
'Cause we all make garbage, and we always will!

1: Now I bet you're askin', bet you're dyin' to see
What a hip hippo hunter from prehistory
Does with garbage! (clap) . . . like old tools of stone—
All that garbage! (clap) . . . like those animal bones.
Well, I throw 'em, I toss 'em, I drop 'em at my feet.
Then I move my camp and go hunt more meat.

2: I'm a wise orator, I'm an ancient Greek.
I was born to talk, and I love to speak
About garbage! (clap) . . . it used to fill our roads—
All that garbage! (clap) . . . now we take it in loads
'Bout a mile beyond our city's limit.
Now our homes and streets aren't buried in it.

3: Now you might be askin' why a British maid
From the Middle Ages would be afraid
Of garbage! (clap) . . . out the window we throw
All our garbage! (clap) . . . to the street below.
Well, our city's so crowded that all of that trash is
Making us sick and giving us rashes.

4: I'm a Spanish explorer and here's what I love:
It's a sailing ship that isn't full of
Garbage! (clap) . . . who wants a messy boat?
All that garbage! (clap) . . . it's tough to stay afloat.
So I toss my trash out into the sea,
Where it disappears and never bothers me.

5: It's the 1860s. I'm a germ detector.
I'm a New York City health inspector.
I hate garbage! (clap) . . . the alleys flow with trash—
All that garbage! (clap) . . . the water's full of ash.
Now those garbage fumes—they can make you ill,
So it's time we cleaned up what we spill.

6: In the Roaring Twenties you would be a grump
If you lived, like me, near an open dump.
It's all garbage! (clap) . . . full of bugs and flies—
In the garbage! (clap) . . . the rats are monster size.
The trash is so high that people say
We'll have garbage mountains 'round here someday.

7: Now we're in the Depression, and some folks feel
That incinerators are the way to deal
With garbage! (clap) . . . it all goes up in smoke—
All that garbage! (clap) . . . but I cough and choke
On the cloudy fumes that fill the air.
I just wish that I could move away somewhere.

8: It's the age of plastics; it's the age of ease.
I'm a '60s chemist, and I'm very pleased
With garbage! (clap) . . . plastic cups, paper plates
In the garbage! (clap) . . . disposables are great.
We've got landfills now to store this waste,
What we throw away can just be replaced.

9: There's an oil crisis, and I have to brag,
'Cause I think I've fixed the biggest snag
With garbage! (clap) . . . 'cause the trash can burn—
All that garbage! (clap) . . . can make a turbine turn.
We'll make energy from our piles of trash.
The only problem will be the toxic ash.

10: I'm your average kid, and I have to say
That I've found an awesome, cleaner way
With garbage! (clap) . . . I try to make much less—
All that garbage! (clap) . . . I'm tired of all this mess.
Now I reuse, recycle, make a compost pile—
It's the garbage shuffle, 1990s style!

Chart 1

Municipal Solid Waste (in millions of tons)						
	1960	1965	1970	1975	1980	1985
generated	87.5	102.3	120.5	125.3	142.6	152.5
recycled	5.8	6.2	8.0	9.1	13.4	15.3
discarded						

Source: Franklin Associates, Ltd.

Chart 2

U.S. Population (in millions)	
1960	180.7
1965	194.3
1970	205.1
1975	216.0
1980	227.8
1985	239.3

Source: U.S. Bureau of Census

Chart 3

Waste Generated (lbs/person/day)	
1960	
1965	
1970	
1975	
1980	
1985	

Chart 4

Composition of Solid Waste (percentage by weight)						
	1960	1965	1970	1975	1980	1985
paper	30.0	33.5	32.4	29.6	32.5	35.5
food & yard	39.4	35.4	32.0	33.2	29.7	29.4
metal	12.8	11.1	12.0	11.5	10.1	9.0
glass	7.8	8.8	11.1	11.4	11.0	8.9
plastic	.5	1.5	2.7	3.8	5.9	7.1
other	9.5	9.6	9.7	10.6	10.7	10.2

Source: Franklin Associates, Ltd.

Chart 5

Composition of Solid Waste (in millions of tons)		
	1960	1985
paper		
food & yard		
metal		
glass		
plastic		

QUESTIONS

1. What percentage of the total amount of solid waste generated was recycled in 1960? In 1985? Many experts think we could recycle more than 25 percent of our municipal solid waste each year. If the United States had recycled 25 percent of this waste in 1985, how many tons of materials would have been recovered?

2. Which materials approximately doubled in weight between 1960 and 1985? Which material showed the greatest rate of increase from 1960 to 1985? How might you explain this dramatic increase?

3. What might you expect to happen to the amount of solid waste generated in a community as the population there increases? Explain your answer. Did the total amount of solid waste generated increase as the population increased in the U.S. between 1960 and 1985? What happened to the average amount of solid waste each person in the United States generated during that time? What factors could possibly have contributed to this?

4. What two categories of waste together consistently make up over half of the municipal solid waste stream by weight? Which material shows a steady increase in percentage over time? Which materials show a general decrease over time? What might explain the decrease in percentage of metal and glass between 1980 and 1985?

5. The information in the charts describes solid waste in terms of weight. What might be a more useful way to measure waste, given that most of it ends up in landfills, that existing landfills are rapidly filling up, and that we're running out of safe places to create new ones? Explain your answer.

(See Tons of Trash—p. 24)

1. Every day for lunch you bring an individual-sized carton of juice that comes wrapped in a handy three-pack. Each carton is easy to carry and comes with its own straw, and you can toss away the empty container when you're done. Your friend tells you that these kinds of juice packages are bad for the environment because they create a lot of unnecessary waste and the materials can't be recycled. **What do you do?**

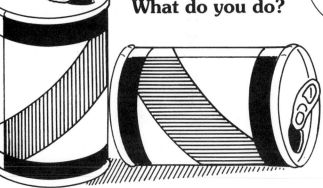

2. At the end of a picnic, your friends start throwing their soda cans into the trash—even though there's a recycling container nearby. When you say something about it, they laugh and call you an enviro-freak. **What do you do?**

4. Your favorite music group just put out a new compact disc. You see the disc hanging on a display rack at the record store. But you notice it's wrapped in a lot of extra throwaway paper and plastic. **What do you do?**

5. Your school is planning to launch hundreds of balloons during a special celebration. You've recently read that released balloons can cause problems for wildlife, especially if the balloons land in the ocean. That's because sea turtles and other animals often mistake the balloons for food. When these animals swallow the balloon scraps, the plastic can block their digestive system and cause them to starve. **What do you do?**

3. You know that the waste problem is serious, and you think recycling is important. But your parents don't seem to have much interest in recycling. **What do you do?**

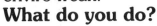

UP IN THE AIR

I f you were asked to define air pollution, what would you say? For mc people, the term "air pollution" is probably synonymous with *smog*—the noxious mixture of water droplets and exhaust fumes or smol particles that's characteristic of big cities the world over. But there's lot more to air pollution than dirty city air. In fact, some of the major environment problems of our time—acid rain, ozone depletion, and the possibility of global clima change, among them—all result from air pollution.

THE FOSSIL FUEL CONNECTION

Turn the key and step on the accelerator. Sparks ignite a mixture of air and the o derived fuel called gasoline, giving life to your car.

Switch on a lamp in a dark room. The room lights up as electricity surges into light bulb—electricity that, in most U.S. homes, comes to us from either a coal- oil-burning power plant.

Pollution from the Past: Coal, oil, and other *fossil fuels* are the source of pow behind a lot of what we do every day. Named for the fact that they formed from th remains of ancient animals and plants, these fuels generate most of the energy use throughout the industrialized world.

Unfortunately, they also generate most of the world's air pollution. That's becau we burn fossil fuels to get the energy out of them. And this *combustion* proce creates a lot of waste, much of it in the form of toxic gases.

The Evil Oxides: Carbon monoxide, carbon dioxide, nitrogen oxides, and sulf dioxide are some of the most dangerous gases produced during fossil fuel combu tion. Of these, carbon monoxide is the most directly harmful to life because i poisonous in very small amounts and it's produced in huge concentrations. contrast, carbon monoxide's "cousin," carbon dioxide (CO_2), is relatively nontoxi But it plays a key role in the greenhouse effect by trapping heat rather than allowir it to escape into space. (See "Changing the Face of the Earth" on page 34 for mo about the greenhouse effect.) The other oxides—sulfur dioxide and nitroge oxides—become most dangerous when they combine with other substance creating problems such as smog and acid rain. (For more about these problems, se "Dangerous Combinations" on the next page.)

Dust in the Wind: Gases aren't the only air pollutants resulting from fossil fu combustion. Tiny bits of dust, metal, soot, and other materials, called *particulate* also find their way into the atmosphere from sources such as diesel engines and pow plants. Particulates can cause respiratory diseases, cancer, and other health pro lems.

Fossil fuel combustion spews out plenty of particulates, but there are also mar other sources of these pollutants. For example, construction projects can kick up lot of dust. And wood-burning stoves and fireplaces can produce large amounts smoke and ash (not to mention carbon dioxide and other gases). So can the burnir of tropical forests. (See "Carbon Collectors" on page 34 for more about air pollutic problems associated with tropical deforestation.)

DANGEROUS COMBINATIONS

It's not just what gets dumped into the air that causes problems; it's also how the individual pollutants interact with each other, water, and/or sunlight. And sometimes pollutants interact with atmospheric conditions—creating problems that, at first glance, might not seem to have much to do with polluted air.

Acid in the Sky: Acid rain is one result of "interactive" pollution. It starts with fossil fuel combustion—mostly from power plants and cars. Sulfur dioxide, originating mainly from coal-burning power plants, and nitrogen oxides, from both power plants and cars, are the gases at fault. Once in the air, these gases combine with water droplets and form sulfuric and nitric acids. The acids can fall as rain or snow, or they can hover near the ground as fog. Acid "rain" can even fall to earth as dry particles. (Although many people use "acid rain" to refer to both wet and dry acid precipitation, some scientists prefer the term "acid deposition.")

Pollution on the Move: The acid in our atmosphere is a perfect example of the interconnectedness that characterizes so many pollution problems. Acid-producing sulfur dioxide that spews out of coal-burning power plants in the Midwest, for instance, often doesn't fall back to earth in the same area. Instead, it's picked up by air currents high in the atmosphere; then it finally falls to the ground, say, in the Adirondack Mountains of New York State. As a result, many of the wilderness lakes in the Adirondacks—once teeming with trout, otters, loons, and other residents typical of healthy mountain lakes in the Northeast—are nearly devoid of life today.

So Much to Learn, So Little Time: There's a lot about acid rain that's still not well understood. For example, many scientists believe that acid rain may be at least partially responsible for killing trees in forests from Canada to the Carolinas. But the mechanisms at work in this destruction are probably incredibly complex. Finding out for certain if acid rain is killing trees could take years. In the meantime, any efforts to pass stronger laws to control acid rain will almost certainly run up against opposition from lobbyists demanding proof of acid rain's guilt. But many researchers feel that coming up with such proof may take too long or may not be possible at all. By the time all the hard facts are in, great stretches of forests—many of which give us timber, maple syrup, and other products—could be long gone. (For more about acid rain, see "Acid Tests" on page 42.)

The Ozone Ogre: Take one hot, summer day, mix in nitrogen oxides and other pollutants from fossil fuel combustion (especially from the exhaust pipes of cars), and sprinkle liberally with sunlight. What do you get? A toxic gas called *ozone.* Hanging like a smoggy shroud over traffic-congested streets and highways, ozone is a pollution plague in many areas. Among other things, it burns your throat, irritates your eyes, damages crops and forests, and causes rubber and other materials to deteriorate.

Same Stuff, Different Place: But ozone isn't always a villain. Fifteen to twenty miles above the earth's surface, it occurs naturally in a zone of the atmosphere called the *stratosphere,* where it blocks out harmful ultraviolet (UV) rays from the sun. Ironically, though, certain human-caused pollutants react with this "good" ozone, causing it to break down. The gases called *chlorofluorocarbons,* or CFCs, are the main culprits. Unlike most other major sources of air pollution, CFCs are not formed from the combustion of fossil fuels. They're used as cooling agents in refrigerators and air conditioners and as propellants in certain products sold as sprays. They're also used in the production of some polystyrene foam products, such as Styrofoam cups and foam packing "peanuts." But when CFCs get into the atmosphere—for example, when the polystyrene foam they're contained in breaks down or when refrigerators or air conditioners develop leaks—they "attack" the ozone layer. The result is *ozone depletion.*

"Holes" in the Heavens: The depletion of ozone has resulted in a thinning of this layer in various places around the world—particularly over Antarctica. Nobody can predict with certainty what the full extent or consequences of ozone depletion will be, but many of the effects of too much harmful UV radiation are well known. Without an adequate ozone shield blocking these rays, say many scientists, stress to the human immune system, crop damage, the number of skin cancer cases, and other UV-related problems will increase. So far, statistics seem to be bearing these predictions out. (See "Holey Ozone!" on page 37 for more about ozone depletion.)

CHANGING THE FACE OF THE EARTH

CFCs are dangerous to the atmosphere in more ways than one. Besides destroying ozone, they also play a role in the *greenhouse effect*—a natural process in which certain gases, known collectively as "greenhouse gases," trap heat that's radiating from the earth's surface. It's as though the earth were inside a giant greenhouse, with the gases acting like the glass walls that allow the sun's radiation in—and then keep the heat it produces from getting out. Under normal circumstances this phenomenon wouldn't be a problem (in fact, it keeps the earth from getting too cold to sustain life). But because people are adding more greenhouse gases to the atmosphere than occur there naturally, many scientists are concerned that we may be drastically changing the atmosphere's chemistry.

Though there are a host of greenhouse gases, including CFCs, one is by far a worse offender than any of the others—mainly because of the sheer quantities of it that human activities generate. That's carbon dioxide (CO_2). Fossil fuel combustion is steadily increasing the percentage of CO_2 in the atmosphere, and so is deforestation—particularly in the tropics.

Carbon Collectors: Tropical deforestation really took off in the mid-1970s. It's mainly an agricultural practice, used to clear land for crops and cattle ranches. Because the burning of large tracts of land is often involved, deforestation releases huge amounts of carbon dioxide that had been stored in jungle trees and other plants.

All plants take in CO_2 from their surroundings and use it in the process of photosynthesis. But the world's rain forests, teeming with vegetation, are gigantic storehouses of carbon. So when we burn down tropical forests, we're hitting the earth's atmosphere with a double whammy: We're adding more heat-trapping CO_2 to the picture, and we're also removing a resource that would otherwise be absorbing some of the extra CO_2 we're pumping into the atmosphere. (For more about tropical deforestation, see *NatureScope—Rain Forests: Tropical Treasures.*)

No Turning Back: "We can't go back if we don't like the new climate." That's what one scientist had to say about the possible long-range effects of the buildup of greenhouse gases. While there's disagreement over what those effects will be, many scientists acknowledge that there's a high probability that the earth's climate is changing because of increasing levels of CO_2 and other greenhouse gases in the atmosphere.

The most widely supported theory examining possible climatic changes claims that we're in for some hot weather ahead. Proponents of this *global warming* theory say that, since CO_2 traps heat, the overall temperature of earth can be expected to increase. And in fact, weather records give some evidence that the average annual temperature of the earth has risen slightly during the last hundred years or so.

Get Out Your Surfboards: A hotter world could be accompanied by a host of negative side effects. And it might not take a big rise in temperature to bring them about. For example, the projected 3 to 10°F increase in overall world temperatures within the next 50 years may not sound drastic, but some scientists say it may be enough to raise sea levels by several feet—enough to flood some coastal cities. And whole agricultural regions, such as the Midwest, could become too hot and dry for many crops.

Put On Your Parkas: Of course, where there's a theory, there's usually a counter-theory. A few people suggest that an increase in atmospheric CO_2 will ultimately cause the earth to cool down. They agree that more CO_2 can be expected to trap more heat, but claim that a warmer climate will cause more moisture to evaporate from the earth's surface. This evaporated moisture could coalesce as clouds high in the atmosphere. More clouds could block out much of the sun's radiation, and the earth might eventually cool down—possibly to the point of entering another ice age.

Terms of Agreement: Trying to understand weather patterns is one of the frustrating parts of the efforts to figure out just how our climate may be changing. An unusually cold winter in a particular region of the country, for example, seems at first glance to run counter to the global warming theory. But paradoxically, this and other weather extremes may be indicative of a change in world weather patterns—and that change may or may not be an overall warming. Because of the uncertainties, many scientists have replaced the term *global warming* with *global climate change*.

What's in Store for Wildlife? The changes thought to be occurring in the earth's climate may happen relatively quickly—too quickly for many lifeforms to adjust. Biologists speculate that, for many species already stressed by habitat loss, poaching, pollution, and other problems, global climate change could be a death sentence. Many of the world's endangered species could lose the struggle to survive.

On the other hand, other species—particularly those that are already common and that have less-specialized needs—might not be affected as drastically by the potential change. And some species would probably find new climatic conditions to be to their advantage.

Time to Take a Hard Look: Although there are a lot of uncertainties surrounding the prospect of global climate change, one thing seems certain: If the world's climate undergoes a major change, the face of the world will change right along with it. And that means that, unless we can slow the pace of the changes our own activities have set in motion, the earth could become a very different world within the span of just a few generations. Now is the time to learn all we can about the nature of these changes—and to take positive action to bring them under control.

WHERE'S THE FRESH AIR?

During a smog alert it's a good idea to stay indoors, right? That depends on whether the air inside is better or worse than the air outside.

Experts are discovering that serious air pollution problems can exist inside houses, offices, schools, and other buildings—a phenomenon that's been labeled "sick building syndrome." The pollutants come from a variety of sources: treated wood, particleboard, and other construction materials; carpets; copy machines; art supplies; cleaning fluids; and heating and cooling systems, to name a few. And they tend to build up in energy-efficient, relatively airtight buildings.

Pollutants such as formaldehyde, nitrogen oxides, carbon monoxide, radon, methylene chloride, and chloroform are some of the common "sick building" troublemakers. As they build up and interact with each other, these and other pollutants are thought to cause health problems ranging from minor irritations such as sore throats to serious diseases such as cancer. Cutting down on the sources of these pollutants and improving ventilation are the best ways to control indoor air pollution. But you can also get help from pollution-fighting plants.

Philodendrons, spider plants, and gerbera daisies are a few of the best pollution fighters.

Something's in the Air

Observe a burning candle; then identify some common sources of air pollution.

Objectives:
Name several sources of air pollution. Explain that burning can release visible and invisible air pollutants.

Ages:
Primary

Materials:
* *copies of page 47*
* *candle and match*
* *white or clear Pyrex dish cover or other heat-resistant glass*
* *crayons or markers*

Subject:
Science

By taking part in this activity, your kids can learn how burning contributes to air pollution and can identify some common sources of air pollution. Begin by having the kids take a deep breath. Ask them to name the "stuff" they're breathing in. (air) Then ask the kids to tell you everything they know about air. During your discussion, you may want to ask questions about what kinds of things need air to live; whether you can see, taste, or feel air; and so on.

Next ask if anyone knows what people mean when they say that air is polluted. Explain that polluted air contains too much of something that can hurt people and other living things. Most air pollution is caused by people burning things. For example, when wood burns in a fireplace, gases and small particles that can pollute the air are released.

Ask the kids to give some examples of air pollution that they've seen. Then ask if they think air pollution can ever be invisible. Discuss their answers, and then tell the kids that they'll be watching a demonstration that shows you can't always see air pollution. Place a candle where everyone can see it and light it. (Blow out the match away from the candle so the smoke doesn't distract the kids.) Ask the kids if they can see any pollution coming from the burning flame. (no) Next lower the glass cover over the candle until it touches the flame. Hold the glass in the flame for a few seconds. Then take away the glass but leave the candle burning.

Have the kids look at the glass and describe what they see. (soot collected on the glass) Explain that as the candle burned, it released gases and very small particles of the burned wax into the air. But the particles weren't visible until they collected on the glass.

Now blow out the candle to show how smoke is produced when the flame goes out. (When you blow out the flame, the temperature of the burning wax drops. At this lower temperature, the burning is not as complete as it was at the higher temperature. The partially burned bits of wax form smoke.)

Next pass out a copy of page 47 to each person and have the kids put an "X" on the things that they think cause air pollution. (If you're working with very young kids, you may want to do the page as a group.) You can also have the kids list the things that cause air pollution that you can see plus things that produce air pollution you might not be able to see. (You would probably see smoke coming from the barbecue, factory, and chimney, but you probably wouldn't see it coming from the car, truck, lawn mower, or jet.)

After the kids have finished, go over the page using the answers below. Be sure to explain that as car, truck, and jet engines work, they burn fuel and release pollutants into the air, but you usually can't see the pollutants that they release. Point out that *all* air pollutants, whether you can see them or not, can affect people's health. For example, air pollution can make people's eyes and throats burn, make it harder for them to breathe, and even give some people heart and lung problems. Polluted air can also make plants grow more slowly.

To finish up, have the kids think of some ways that people could help reduce air pollution. (drive cars less, use fireplaces less, encourage development of solar-powered cars, and so on) Also see chapter five for more ideas on how kids can help reduce pollution.

ANSWERS: car, jet, truck, factory, barbecue, lawn mower, chimney

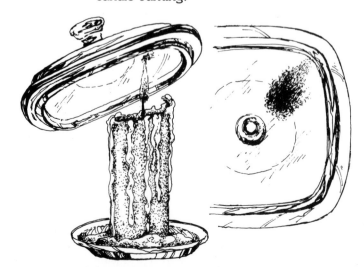

Holey Ozone!

Look at a cartoon and listen to a story about how CFCs affect the ozone layer, and then illustrate facts about ozone and CFCs with some original cartoons.

Objectives:
Name several sources of CFCs. Describe how CFCs affect the ozone layer.

Ages:
Intermediate

Materials:
- *copies of page 48*
- *crayons or colored markers*
- *drawing paper*

Subjects:
Science and Art

ACTION TIP!

CFC CONTROL

- Avoid using and buying products that might be made with CFCs. For example, use a reusable cup instead of a plastic foam one. If you're not sure if CFCs are in a product, ask the retailer. Even if they don't know, you'll be informing them that consumers are concerned about CFCs.
- When servicing your car, take it to a station that can recycle the air-conditioning coolant and keep CFCs from being released into the atmosphere.
- Have home and car air conditioners checked for leaks.

Cartoons can make even "heavy science" easier to understand—and to remember. By looking at a cartoon as they listen to a story, your kids can get a better idea of how CFCs (chlorofluorocarbons) affect the ozone layer.

Start by using the background information on pages 33-34 to tell the kids about the ozone layer and how it absorbs harmful ultraviolet rays from the sun. Also explain that scientists have discovered that CFCs are destroying the ozone layer. Then pass out a copy of page 48 to each person and explain that the cartoon characters represent CFCs (circles) and ozone molecules (triangles). Tell the kids that you'll be reading a story that explains more about what is happening on the page. Encourage the kids to listen carefully because they'll be using the information later on. (In the story, we've simplified some of the information about how CFCs affect ozone. See "More About the Ozone Layer and CFCs" on page 38 for a more detailed explanation.)

After you read "The Ozone Story" (see below), answer any questions the kids may have, using the information on page 38. Make sure they understand that the special conditions over Antarctica worsen the effects that CFCs have on the ozone layer in that region. You can also discuss how people can help protect the ozone layer.

Then pass out drawing paper and crayons or markers, and tell the kids that they'll have a chance to create their own cartoon stories that illustrate some aspect of the CFC/ozone problem. They can either incorporate the ozone and CFC characters from page 48 into their cartoons, or they can make up their own cartoon characters. For example, they could illustrate a CFC molecule's description of how it attacks the ozone layer.

THE OZONE STORY

Hi! I'm an ozone molecule. I spend my time about 15 miles above the earth, soaking up ultraviolet rays from the sun before they zap you people on earth. We ozone molecules take a lot of pride in our work. But something's been happening to us. There aren't as many ozone molecules as there used to be. And I'm here to tell you why.

You see, it all started when you people began using chemicals called CFCs. You may not realize it, but you probably use something made with CFCs just about every day. You can see some of these products, such as the plastic foam plates, scattered on the ground. CFCs are used to make the coolants that are in refrigerators and air conditioners. They're used to make computer parts. And CFCs are used to make some plastic foam cups, plates, and other containers.

But CFCs don't stay in those products forever. Look at the old cars in that junkyard—there are loads of CFCs leaking out of the old air conditioners. CFCs also leak out of plastic foam cups and plates as

the foam slowly breaks apart. And see that plastic foam factory over there? Lots of CFCs leak into the air as plastic foam is being made.

Once they get into the air, CFCs slowly drift higher and higher. In fact, it may take them 10 or 15 years to get way up here where I am. But the longer, the better, as far as I'm concerned. Because once CFCs get near us ozone molecules—well, that's when the trouble begins.

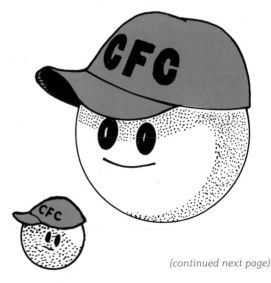

(continued next page)

Before CFCs get up here to the ozone layer where we ozone molecules hang out, they're protected from the sun's powerful ultraviolet rays. That's because me and my ozone pals soak up these ultraviolet rays. But when those CFCs drift through us ozone molecules and come out *above* the ozone layer . . . WHAM! They get zapped by those rays! And a terrible change takes place in the CFCs. They become OZONE EATERS! You can see ultraviolet rays hitting some of the CFCs that just drifted above the ozone layer.

Once CFCs become ozone eaters, they can do a lot of damage. Why, I've heard some of those big-mouthed ozone eaters brag that they've destroyed 100,000 ozone molecules! And as more of us ozone molecules are destroyed, the ozone layer is becoming thinner, and more harmful ultraviolet rays are reaching the earth. And that means trouble for you people on earth.

The ozone molecules over Antarctica have really big problems. Down there, the super-cold temperatures make lots of ozone eaters form. I've heard that during some parts of the year, almost half of the Antarctic ozone molecules get eaten. I'm sure glad I don't live there!

Well, that's the end of my story. Now that you know what's happening up here, I sure hope you'll do something to help us ozone molecules. After all, we've been saving your skin for years!

MORE ABOUT THE OZONE LAYER AND CFCs

Ozone Dynamics: Ozone is a form of oxygen. Ozone molecules can be found from 15 to 20 miles above the earth, with the peak concentration (the ozone layer) occurring at about 15 miles. Although ozone absorbs most of the ultraviolet (UV) rays from the sun, it makes up only a very small fraction of the atmosphere.

The ozone supply is constantly being recycled. When an ozone molecule absorbs UV light, the molecule splits apart. A new ozone molecule soon forms from the "old parts." If left undisturbed, this cycle maintains a balance of ozone in the atmosphere.

CFCs Enter the Picture: Chlorofluorocarbons, or CFCs, were invented in 1930. Many different kinds of CFCs have been developed since then. Because they are so stable (that is, they won't easily react with other chemicals) and nontoxic, CFCs have been used to make a variety of products, such as aerosol propellants, coolants, and plastic foam. (Some plastic foam products are now being made with CFC-substitutes, but there's no way to distinguish these products from those made with CFC-containing foam. And many CFC substitutes, such as HCFCs, also harm the ozone layer.)

Ozone Wreckers: As a CFC molecule drifts above the ozone layer, it's bombarded by the UV rays of the sun. This splits apart the CFC molecule, releasing an atom of chlorine, which in turn "attacks" an ozone molecule. The chlorine atom breaks apart the ozone molecule in a such a way that it can't recombine to form a new ozone molecule. This disrupts the ozone cycle, resulting in a net loss of ozone.

Scientists have found that a single chlorine atom can destroy up to 100,000 ozone molecules before it becomes inactive or drifts down into the lower atmosphere. This means that introducing just a small quantity of CFCs into the atmosphere can have a big effect on the ozone layer. Scientists have also found that some types of CFCs are more harmful than others, because they last longer in the atmosphere (about 100 years) and release more chlorine molecules.

Polar Perils: From June to August, the extremely cold winter temperatures over Antarctica help to foster the formation of chlorine molecules, and create a temporary but extreme thinning of the ozone layer. By September, a "hole" the size of the U.S. may form. Ozone levels may drop by as much as 50 percent in the annual Antarctic ozone hole. This hole disappears when temperatures warm up around late November.

Ozone Around the World: In contrast to the severe ozone depletion over Antarctica, scientists have found that Arctic ozone levels drop by only 5 to 10 percent during the winter. This less drastic depletion is related to the shorter, warmer Arctic winters. Scientists have also detected a 2- to 3-percent drop in average worldwide ozone levels. Some scientists believe that because of this ozone depletion, more of the sun's harmful UV rays are reaching the earth. Many scientists feel this is responsible for a rise in the number of cases of skin cancer.

Saving the Ozone: Alarmed by warnings from scientists, the U.S. and a few other nations banned the use of CFCs in most aerosols in 1978. Then, in 1985, the announcement of the Antarctic ozone "hole" spurred governments to work together to cut worldwide use of CFCs. Countries eventually agreed to phase out CFCs altogether by the year 2000 and to help less developed countries find alternatives to CFCs. (See page 70 for more about this agreement, called the Montreal Protocol.)

Until CFCs are phased out, consumers should be particularly careful to avoid products made with the following types of CFCs. Although all CFCs damage the ozone layer to some extent, these CFCs are particularly harmful:
• trichlorofluoromethane (CFC-11)
• dichlorodifluoromethane (CFC-12)
• trichlorotrifluoroethane (CFC-113)
• dichlorotetrafluoroethane (CFC-114)
Consumers should also be on the lookout for products containing HCFCs.

The Awful Eight

Put on a play about eight major air pollutants.

Objectives:
Name some of the major air pollutants, describe what produces them, and discuss some of the effects they have on people and the environment.

Ages:
Intermediate and Advanced

Materials:
* *copies of the play on pages 49, 50, and 51*
* *large pieces of posterboard*
* *yardsticks*
* *markers*
* *materials for making costumes and props (optional)*

Subjects:
Science and Drama

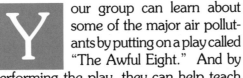

Your group can learn about some of the major air pollutants by putting on a play called "The Awful Eight." And by performing the play, they can help teach other people about the pollution problems in our atmosphere.

Before you put on the play, use the background information on pages 32-35 to discuss the major air pollutants and the problems they cause. Then assign each part under the "Cast of Characters" below and pass out copies of the play on pages 49-51. (You can adjust the number of characters to fit the size of your group.) Give the kids time to learn their lines, design cos-

tumes, and plan any special effects they might want to add.

After the kids perform the play, review the eight major air pollutants by having each "pollutant" (or group) come out and take a bow. The pollutants should state their name; what causes them; how they affect people, wildlife, and the environment; and what people can do to help reduce this type of pollution. Or you can have the audience supply this information to see how much they learned from watching "The Awful Eight."

(This play is adapted with permission from "The Big, Bad Six" by Carolyn Duckworth, *Ranger Rick,* September 1987, pp 22-29.)

CAST OF CHARACTERS

The number of characters and some suggestions for props and costumes are in parentheses.

Connie Lung, reporter (props—microphone, notebook)
Harry Wheezer, reporter (props—microphone, notebook)
The Particulates (3; prop—dirt; costume—dirty jeans and brown t-shirts, smear dirt on face)
Carbon Monoxide (1; costume—sneakers, hat, trenchcoat, and sunglasses)
The Toxics (5; props—gasoline cans made from cardboard, skull-and-crossbones symbols worn around neck; costume—black clothing)
Sulfur Dioxide (1; prop—water gun or spray bottle filled with water; costume—

torn t-shirt, yellow and white streamers attached to clothing)
Nitrogen Oxides (Nitros) (5; props—dead branches; costume—each Nitro can wear one of the letters in "nitro")
Bad Ozone (1; costume—sunglasses, sophisticated clothing for a "big city look")
Good Ozone (1; costume—sunglasses and light-colored clothing with bits of cotton attached to represent clouds)
Chlorofluorocarbons (CFCs) (4; prop—plastic foam packing "peanuts"; costume—foam fast-food containers and foam cups or "peanuts" attached to clothing)
EPA Scientists (2; prop—notebooks)
Carbon Dioxide (2; costume—t-shirts and shorts, black costume makeup wiped on clothing, legs, and faces)

DIRTY AIR! LET'S KEEP IT THAT WAY!

TIPS FOR PUTTING ON THE PLAY

* Have the "pollutants" make picket signs by taping large pieces of posterboard to yardsticks and writing slogans on the posterboard. (See slogan suggestions in the description of the play's setting on page 49.)
* If your space is limited, have only some of the pollutants picket at a time.
* If some kids prefer nonspeaking roles, you can let them carry picket signs or be camera people filming the report. They could

also take on the responsibilities of stage manager, costume designer, or set designer.
* Go over these pronunciations with the kids playing the Toxics: benzene (BEN-zeen), xylene (ZI-leen), toluene (TOL-you-een).
* If your audience is small, have Harry and Connie come up with some ways that people can help reduce air pollution at the end of the play.

Pollution Pathways

Map the dispersal of radioactive air pollutants released by an explosion at the Chernobyl nuclear power plant.

Objectives:
Describe how air pollution travels from one area to another. Locate cities and countries on a map.

Ages:
Intermediate and Advanced

Materials:
- *large world map*
- *copies of pages 52 and 53*
- *bulletin board*
- *pushpins*
- *atlases and/or world maps*

Subjects:
Science and Geography

There are no state or national boundaries in the atmosphere. Winds can carry pollutants hundreds or even thousands of miles from their origin, creating air pollution in other regions. By tracing the movement of radiation released during an accident at the Chernobyl nuclear power plant, your kids will see how air pollution can become a global issue.

Before you get started, hang a large world map on a bulletin board. (Later, you'll be using pushpins to mark different places on the map.) Then begin by asking the kids to name some sources of air pollution. Explain that as weather systems move through an area, winds pick up and carry air pollutants. Eventually these pollutants fall from the sky as dry particles, or they are washed back to earth by rain, snow, or fog. Also explain that, in general, the distance air pollutants travel depends on how high in the atmosphere they go. Pollutants that don't rise very high tend to be deposited relatively close to their source. But pollutants that are lifted high in the atmosphere may travel thousands of miles before they drop back to earth.

Next point out the location of the Chernobyl nuclear power plant on a world map (see page 53), and use the information under "Explosion at Chernobyl" on the next page to tell the kids about the accident. Explain that the radioactive gases and particles released by the explosion formed a toxic cloud that soon split into two parts. Point out that the plant released radiation for 10 days after the explosion, and since the winds shifted several times during this period, radiation was carried in many different directions. By tracking the radioactive particles and gases released by the explosion, scientists learned a lot about how air pollutants travel from place to place. (See the maps below for an illustration of where the radiation traveled.)

Now pass out a copy of page 52 to each person and explain that each of the 29 "Pollution Points" on the page describes when the radioactive cloud from Chernobyl reached a certain location. The points are grouped under the headings of Day 2, Day 3, and so on. This indicates how many days after the explosion it took the radioactive cloud to reach a certain location. For example, the radiation reached Stockholm, Sweden, on April 28, the third day after the explosion. (*Note:* The information on page 52 doesn't include *all* the countries that received radiation from Chernobyl, and in some cases, the dates indicating when radiation reached certain areas are approximations.)

Next split the group into two teams and explain that the members of each team will be working together to map the "Pollution Points." Mark Chernobyl's location with a pushpin on the world map. Have the teams gather close to the map and explain that the mapping will start with someone from the first team reading pollution point 1 out loud. He or she will have 40 seconds to find that city on the map and mark it with a pushpin. Team members can help the player by giving directional tips, such as "move closer to Spain," but they can't point to any specific location on the map. If the team member finds the point within 40 seconds, his or her team gets one point. If not, the other team gets a chance to find the

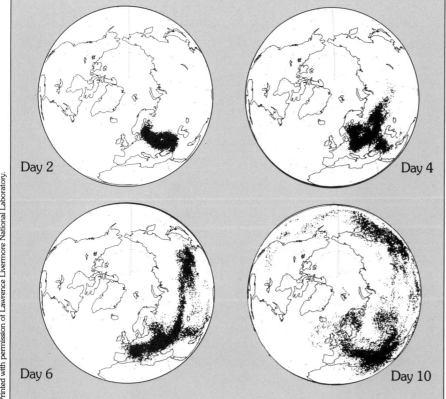

Day 2

Day 4

Day 6

Day 10

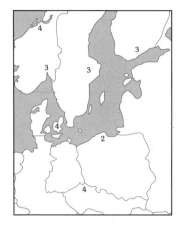

correct location. Have the teams take turns locating the points until all 29 points have been mapped.

Next give each person a copy of page 53 and set out some atlases and/or world maps. Tell the kids that they'll plot some of the points on the Copycat Page so that they'll have a record of where much of the radiation released from Chernobyl traveled. They can use the atlases and world maps to help them find the points. (Tell the kids that, because of the limited area shown on their maps, they'll be able to plot only the first 22 points.) Have the kids write in the number of the day for each location (not the number of the pollution point). This way their maps will show how far the pollution traveled within a certain number of days. For example, when they plot pollution point 1, they'll write a small number "2" where Gdansk is located in Poland.

After the kids have finished mapping, ask them to describe how rainfall affected the amount of radiation that fell on certain areas. (More radiation reached the ground in areas where it rained.) Point out to the kids that "pollution on the move" also causes problems in the U.S. Use the information on page 33 to discuss how pollutants produced by coal-burning power plants in the Midwest contribute to acid rain that falls in the eastern U.S. and Canada. Explain that acid rain-causing pollutants pour out of smokestacks that are sometimes more than 1000 feet tall. These tall stacks were built to reduce air pollution problems near the plants. Unfortunately, the tall-stack solution created pollution problems for other regions. The stacks shoot the pollutants high in the atmosphere, where they're picked up by high-altitude winds. These winds may carry the pollutants thousands of miles away, resulting in acid rain in other regions.

EXPLOSION AT CHERNOBYL

The Big Blast: On April 26, 1986, at 1:23 AM, Chernobyl became the site of the world's worst nuclear power plant accident. Operators were shutting down one of the reactors for maintenance when the power suddenly surged and the reactor exploded. The blast blew the reactor apart and sent radioactive gases and particles as high as 3 miles into the atmosphere. Two plant workers were killed by the explosion. Later 29 others died from radiation exposure.

Within days, more than 120,000 people were evacuated from an 18-mile radius around the plant. As fires inside the reactor burned, helicopters dumped tons of lead, sand, and other minerals on the flames. Despite these efforts, the fires burned for 10 days after the blast, continuing to release radioactive pollutants into the air.

Where It Went: The explosion resulted in a huge cloud that soon split into two parts. One part of the cloud moved northwest toward Poland and Scandinavia, and then southwest across central Europe. The other part of the cloud moved east, across Asia, over Japan and the North Pacific, and eventually reached western North America. (The "Pollution Points" on page 52 track the movement of both parts of the cloud.) And as the reactor continued to burn, it released radiation that moved south and east of the plant. But scientists believe that, in most cases, the amounts of radiation deposited outside the Soviet Union were relatively low.

Effects of the Explosion: The first few weeks following the Chernobyl blast were filled with confusion. Some European countries ordered the destruction of millions of dollars worth of contaminated produce, milk, and livestock. But in other nearby European countries, people were told that there was no danger and that it was safe to consume these products. Farmers suffered huge financial losses when countries in other parts of the world refused to import produce from Europe.

The explosion also strained relations between the Soviet Union and other nations. Many countries were angered by the Soviet Union's delay in reporting the accident (officials didn't announce it until April 29).

Chernobyl's Legacy: The damaged reactor at Chernobyl now stands entombed in thick layers of concrete and steel, while the other reactors at the plant are again producing energy. But the disaster is still taking its toll. Some scientists predict that within the next few decades, thousands of people who were exposed to the radiation could develop cancer.

Acid Tests

Conduct several demonstrations to find out about the effects of acid rain.

Objectives:
Give an example of an acid and a base. Explain why some soils are not affected by acid rain as much as others. Describe how acid rain can affect plants, animals, and buildings and other structures. Discuss some methods that can help reduce the effects of acid rain.

Ages:
Intermediate and Advanced

Materials:
- *chalkboard or easel paper*
- *copies of the demonstrations on pages 44 and 45*
- *see demonstrations for other materials*

Subject:
Science

Your kids can do some demonstrations to learn about how acid rain affects the environment. Start the activity by explaining to the kids how acid rain forms (see the background information on page 33). Then give each person a copy of "Acid Demonstrations" on pages 44 and 45. Tell the kids that by doing several demonstrations, they'll learn more about the effects of acid rain. The first demonstration will help them learn about the *pH scale*.

Explain that the pH scale is a simple way to measure the relative acidity of a substance. The scale ranges from 0 to 14. A solution with a pH of 1 is very acidic, while one with a pH of 12 or 13 is very basic, or alkaline. A solution with a pH of 7 is considered neutral. For example, rainwater, which is normally slightly acidic, averages between 5.0 and 5.6. The pH scale is logarithmic, which means that there is a tenfold difference between numbers. A solution that has a pH of 4 is about 10 times more acidic than a solution with a pH of 5.

Also explain to the kids that they'll be using specially treated pH paper to measure the acidity of different liquids. When they dip the paper into a liquid, it will turn a certain color. They should immediately match this color to a color chart to find out the pH. You might want to take the pH of one of the liquids listed in demonstration 1 as a group to make sure the kids understand how to use pH paper. (*Note:* Although pH paper is not the most accurate measurement of acidity, it does measure relative acidity, which is what's important for these demonstrations.)

Next divide the kids into small groups and have them do demonstration 1. Afterward copy the names of all the test solutions on a chalkboard or sheet of easel paper and have the groups fill in their results so the kids can see what the other groups came up with. Then, once the kids understand the pH scale, have them tackle the other demonstrations. You may want to have the kids work in teams to do all the demonstrations, or you can have the members of each team do one demonstration and later explain their results to the group. Also have the kids

write down their answers to "What Happened?" and "Think About It" so they can discuss each demonstration later. See the information under "Acid Test Follow-Up" on the next page to add to your discussion. You might also want to have the kids point out the control in demonstrations 2-5.

Supply Tips
- You can order pH paper from biological supply companies, including Carolina Biological Supply, 2700 York Rd., Burlington, NC 27215, 800-334-5551. Be sure to order wide-range (1-12 or 0-14) pH hydrion paper. You'll need 4 or 5 rolls for a group of 25.
- You can get powdered lime, potting soil, and sphagnum moss at nurseries and garden stores. Be sure that the potting soil you get has a pH of around 6. You might want to buy a soil pH test kit to check the pH of the potting soil.
- Be sure to buy chalk that has calcium carbonate in it.
- Use reusable or recyclable containers for the demonstrations.

Safety Tips
- Caution the kids to avoid getting the powdered lime near their eyes or mouths. Also be sure to have them wash their hands after doing the demonstrations.

ACTION TIP!

TAKE A LOCAL ACID TEST

Your kids can monitor the rain in their area to see if it's acidic, and then exchange their information with other people around the country. Contact the National Geographic Society at 800-368-2728 to find out more about "Kidsnet," a computerized acid rain information exchange program. And for information about an acid rain monitoring program sponsored by the National Audubon Society, write to the Citizens Acid Rain Monitoring Network, 950 Third Ave, New York, NY, 10022.

1. Lemon juice—2, vinegar— 2 or 3, cola soft drink—4, coffee—5, tap water—5, milk—6, distilled water—6 or 7, baking soda and water—7, liquid antacid—9 or 10, lime and water—12. Some kids may have gotten different pH readings because they interpreted the colors on the pH scale differently or because there were variations in the pH paper.

2. The seeds watered with distilled water should have sprouted first and grown the most. The seeds watered with the acidic solution should have sprouted later or not at all. (If they did sprout, they might have had yellowed and/or stunted leaves.)

The plants were kept inside to keep rainwater from affecting the results of the experiment. Watering several seeds with each type of solution reduced the likelihood of any one seed skewing the results because of disease or other problems.

The kids should have come up with the idea that acid rain (represented by the vinegar-and-water solution) can negatively affect plant growth. Be sure to point out to the kids that the vinegar solution only *simulates* the acidity of acid rain. Since vinegar contains substances that are not found in acid rain, the growth of the seeds may have been influenced by the other ingredients in vinegar, as well as by the acid in the solution. Also point out that acid rain is rarely as acidic as the solution used in this demonstration. (Acid rain generally has a pH of about 4.)

Scientists think that acid rain doesn't significantly affect most crops, since these plants are exposed to acid rain for a relatively short time and because the soil they grow in is usually limed to reduce acidity and fertilized to replenish nutrients. But some scientists think that acid rain may affect trees (which are longer lived and can be exposed to acid rain for many years) by weakening them and making them more vulnerable to stress. For example, acid rain may increase a tree's susceptibility to drought, disease, cold, and insect attack. Acid rain may also cause certain essential minerals in the soil to dissolve and wash out. Without these minerals, a tree may grow more slowly. These effects can be worsened when acid rain combines with other pollutants, such as ozone.

3. The pH of the water should have become lower after the acidic ice cubes melted, while the pH of the water with the distilled-water ice cubes should not have changed.

The surge of acidic water from sudden snowmelt (represented by the ice cubes made from the acidic solution) can cause a drastic drop in pH. This sudden jump in acidity (called "spring shock") can kill certain species of fish. Spring shock also interferes with the reproduction of fish and other aquatic animals. For example, most fish, salamanders, and frogs lay their eggs in the early spring—just about the time spring shock occurs. The eggs and young of these species are very sensitive to acidity and are often killed by the sudden increase in acidity. And if the eggs survive, the young that hatch may be deformed.

4. The kids should have noticed bubbling when they added the acid solution to the chalk. The bubbles formed as the acid in the solution reacted with the calcium carbonate in the chalk. They should have seen much less bubbling when they added distilled water to the chalk. Overnight, the chalk in the acid solution should have partially dissolved, and the carved line should have become much less distinct. The chalk in the distilled water should have been less affected, and the carved line should not have changed much in appearance.

As acid rain falls on marble structures, the acid slowly dissolves the marble. (Be sure to point out that most rainfall isn't as acidic as the solution the kids made up in this demonstration. But, over time, acid rain does erode buildings, statues, and other structures.)

5. The pH of the solution poured through the sphagnum moss should have stayed the same. The solution poured through the potting soil should have become less acidic. Results for the soil taken from your area will vary, depending on the pH of your soil. The potting soil, which is significantly less acidic than the solution, acted as a buffer; it neutralized some of the acid in the solution. The sphagnum moss is more acidic and didn't neutralize the acids in the solution. If the pH of the solution poured through the soil from your area remained the same, your soil is probably acidic; if the pH increased, your soil is probably alkaline.

If you added lime to your soil, the pH of the solution that drained through the funnel should increase. That's because adding lime to soil makes it more alkaline and helps it to neutralize the acidic solution.

Differences in soil types can help explain the varying effects of acid rain. In areas with deep, alkaline soils, acidic rainwater slowly trickles through the soil and is neutralized before it reaches lakes and streams. Other areas, such as some parts of New England and the Adirondacks, have thin, relatively acidic soils. Acid rain quickly runs into lakes and streams without being neutralized. Because of this, many lakes in these regions have become acidified.

6. The kids should have come up with the idea of adding lime or baking soda to the water to make it less acidic. (Lime will be most effective in small amounts, since it is more alkaline than baking soda.)

In some areas, people have added lime pellets or powder to lakes to make them less acidic. Although this has been relatively successful in some cases, it is an expensive and short-term solution. If acid rain continues to fall, more lime will have to be added in a year or two. Scientists agree that the best way to combat acid rain is to stop it at its source. Problems to consider include how adding lime or baking soda could affect aquatic life and how to figure out the correct amount of lime or baking soda to add.

(continued next page)

#1: SETTING UP THE SCALE

What You'll Need: pH paper, 10 small containers, masking tape, markers, vinegar, lemon juice, tap water, milk, cola soft drink, coffee, distilled water, liquid antacid, baking-soda-and-water solution (1/4 teaspoon baking soda in 2/3 cup water), powdered-lime-and-water solution (1/4 teaspoon lime in 2/3 cup water)

What to Do:

1. Place a small sample of each liquid in a separate container. Label each container with the name of the liquid, using masking tape and a marker.
2. Test the pH of each liquid by dipping a 1 1/2" piece of pH paper in the liquid. (Be careful to throw away the used pH paper, since it can stain desktops and other surfaces. Also be sure to use a new strip of pH paper each time you test a liquid.) Record the pH for each liquid.

What Happened? List the liquids in order from most acidic to least acidic. Compare your results with those of the other groups.

Think About It: Did everyone get the same answers? If not, why do you think some of your answers differed?

#2: TO GROW OR NOT TO GROW

What You'll Need: Seeds (radish, clover, pea, or mustard seeds will work best), large container, distilled water, 20 empty pint milk cartons, potting soil, marker, masking tape, vinegar, ruler, measuring cup, pH paper

What to Do:

1. Fill the 20 milk cartons three-quarters full with potting soil. Plant one seed in each carton.
2. Label 10 of the cartons with "A" for acid and 10 with "DW" for distilled water.
3. Make a solution with a pH of about 3 by mixing 1 cup of vinegar with 4 cups of distilled water.
4. Measure the pH of the distilled water and record it. Then water the seeds in the cartons labeled "DW" with distilled water and the seeds in the cartons labeled "A" with the acidic solution. Put the cartons in a sunny spot indoors.
5. Over the next three weeks or so, water all the seedlings with the appropriate kind of water whenever they look dry. Make sure you give each seedling the same amount of water. Record the date each seed sprouts and also measure the heights of the seedlings every few days.

What Happened? Which seedlings grew the most? Which grew the least?

Think About It: Why was it important to keep the seedlings indoors instead of letting them grow outside? Why do you think you were told to water more than one seed with each solution? If acid rain has about the same acidity as the acid solution you used, how might it affect plant growth?

#3: THE BIG CHILL

What You'll Need: 2 ice cube trays, distilled water, lemon juice, freezer, pH paper, 2 containers, marker, masking tape, measuring spoon and cup

What to Do:

1. Take the pH of the distilled water and record it. Then pour enough distilled water into an ice tray to make 3 ice cubes. Label the tray "DW" for distilled water and put it in the freezer.
2. Add 1 1/2 teaspoons of lemon juice to 2/3 cup of distilled water to make a solution with a pH of 3. Pour enough of the lemon-juice solution into an ice tray to make 3 ice cubes. Label the tray with "A" for acid and put it in the freezer.
3. Once the ice cubes have formed, pour the same amount of distilled water (about 3 cups) into each container.
4. Put the 3 distilled-water ice cubes into one of the containers and let them melt. Then put the 3 ice cubes made from the acidic solution into the other container and let them melt.
5. After the ice cubes melt, stir both solutions. Then take the pH of the liquid in each container and record the results.

What Happened? What was the pH of the water in each of the containers after the ice cubes melted?

Think About It: In some areas, acid snow falls during the winter. In early spring, the snow that has fallen throughout the winter melts and runs into lakes and streams. Using the results of this demonstration, how might the acidic snowmelt affect the pH of lakes and streams? What other effects might this change in pH have?

#4: CHALK TALK

What You'll Need: pH paper, lemon juice, distilled water, 2 equal-sized pieces of chalk, 2 small containers, paper clip, masking tape, marker, measuring cup and spoon

What to Do:

1. Take the pH of the distilled water and record it.
2. Make up a solution with a pH of 3 by adding 1 1/2 teaspoons of lemon juice to 2/3 cup of distilled water.
3. Unbend a paper clip, and then use it to carve a line in one piece of chalk. Place the chalk in one container and add enough acidic solution to cover the chalk. Observe and record what happens, and then label this container "A" for acid.
4. Carve an identical line in the other piece of chalk, and then place it in the other container. Add enough distilled water to cover the chalk. Observe and record what happens, and then label this container "DW."
5. Let the chalk remain in the solutions for 24 hours.
6. When the 24 hours are up, pour out the liquids and take a close look at each piece of chalk.

What Happened? Is there any difference between the two pieces of chalk? Explain your answer.

Think About It: Many statues and buildings are made from marble. Marble is made up of the same minerals as chalk is, but it's harder than chalk. Using the results of this demonstration, what do you think could be happening to marble statues and buildings that are located in areas where acid rain falls?

#5: SOIL STUFF

What You'll Need: sample of soil from your area, potting soil, sphagnum moss, powdered lime, funnel, filter paper, vinegar, distilled water, measuring cup, large container, pH paper

What to Do:

1. Make up a solution with a pH of about 3 by adding 1 cup of vinegar to 3 cups distilled water. Record the pH.
2. Put a piece of filter paper into a funnel, and then fill the funnel about two-thirds full with the sphagnum moss.
3. Put the funnel over a large container, and then pour the acidic solution into the funnel (make sure you don't add too much liquid all at once). Wait until all the liquid has collected in the container below the funnel.
4. Take the pH of the liquid that collects in the container.
5. After rinsing out the funnel and container and

removing the used filter paper, repeat the experiment twice using potting soil instead of sphagnum moss and then using the soil from your area. (Be sure to rinse the equipment between uses.)

What Happened? Did the pH of the liquid change after you poured it through the sphagnum moss? The potting soil? The soil from your area?

Think About It: Based on your results, what do you think would happen if you added a small amount of lime to the soil from your area, and then poured some of the acidic solution through it? In some areas where acid rain falls, lakes and streams don't show the effects of acid rain. But in other areas where acid rain falls, lakes and streams have become acidified. Based on the results of this demonstration, why do you think these differences exist?

#6: BACK TO BASICS
What You'll Need: tap water, pH paper, container, vinegar, measuring spoon, baking soda, powdered lime, vinegar or lemon juice, distilled water

What to Do:
1. Put some tap water in a container and measure the pH.
2. Add a small amount of vinegar to the water and measure the pH again. Keep adding vinegar until the solution has a pH of 4.
3. What could you do to return the pH of the water to its original pH? (Think about the substances you tested in demonstration 1.) Your goal is to "fix" the pH by adding only a small amount of one substance.

What Happened? Did your experiment successfully return the solution to its original pH? Describe what you did.

Think About It: Using the results of this demonstration, what are some steps you might take to decrease the acidity in an acidic lake? What kinds of problems might this action cause?

A Heated Controversy

Read and discuss two articles about global climate change.

Objectives:
Discuss the causes and possible effects of global climate change. Explain why it's important for individuals to be aware of current issues in science.

Ages:
Advanced

Materials:
• copies of pages 54 and 55

Subjects:
Science, Social Studies, and Language Arts

By reading two articles about global climate change, your kids can learn more about how some air pollutants may be affecting our climate. Begin by asking the kids to tell you what they know about global climate change, often referred to as "global warming." Then use the background information under "Changing the Face of the Earth" on page 34 to talk about the greenhouse effect and greenhouse gases, such as carbon dioxide and CFCs.

Next explain that although most scientists agree that the increasing amounts of carbon dioxide, CFCs, methane, and other greenhouse gases in the atmosphere will affect the world's climate, there's some disagreement about whether these changes have already begun and how serious the effects will be. Scientists also disagree on how we should react to global climate change.

Now pass out paper and copies of pages 54 and 55 to each person and explain that each of these articles expresses a point of view about global climate change. (Neither article was written by a real scientist, but both points of view have been expressed by people in the scientific community.) Give the kids time to read the articles and answer the questions that follow the second one. Afterward discuss the kids' answers using the information under "Is the Heat Really On?" and "A Look at the Facts" on page 46. Finish up by having the kids brainstorm some ways that they can help reduce the amount of greenhouse gases that are being released into the atmosphere. (bike, walk, carpool, or take public transportation whenever possible and encourage friends and family to do the same; conserve electricity and buy energy-efficient appliances; don't buy products made with CFCs; encourage parents to have car air conditioners serviced at stations that can recycle coolant made with CFCs and to have home and car air conditioners checked for leaks)

(continued next page)

IS THE HEAT REALLY ON?

1. Scientist 1 thinks that global warming is already underway and we need to cut carbon dioxide and CFC emissions now to slow it. Scientist 2 believes that we can't be sure yet if the world's climate is warming as a result of increased CFC and carbon dioxide levels and that we need to do more research before we take any drastic action.

2. *Advantages:* would help cut down on the possibility of causing further global warming; would cut down on pollution in general due to decreasing use of fossil fuels, increasing energy efficiency, and switching to alternative energy; would save money due to use of more energy-efficient appliances.

Disadvantages: would cost more in the short run to develop more energy-efficient cars, factories, and appliances; might eliminate some jobs or cut profits.

3. *Advantages:* would result in more knowledge about our atmosphere; would cost less in the short term; would not inflict hardships on U.S. businesses and people in developing countries.

Disadvantages: would not reduce pollution; would cost more in the long run; would increase the likelihood that, later on, it might be too late to stop the warming trend. (*Note:* Point out that the costs associated with either scientist's recommendation are difficult to estimate.)

4. A possible compromise could include making some of the changes suggested by Scientist 1 to help increase energy conservation, while continuing to do research as Scientist 2 advocated. Some scientists and policymakers support this strategy to slow the potential warming trend without threatening to harm the economies of the U.S. and other countries.

5. Opinions will vary. Point out that decisions about global climate change, like decisions about many complicated environmental issues, are often based on information that may or may not be as complete as people would like. People's values also influence their decisions.

6. It's important to stay informed about scientific issues so that you can better understand problems and can change your daily behaviors to help solve problems. For example, consumers can avoid buying products that contribute to the buildup of greenhouse gases, if they know what the problems associated with these gases are and how their actions contribute to the problems. And people can write to their representatives to encourage them to support environmental legislation.

A LOOK AT THE FACTS

- Overall, average world temperatures have risen by about 1°F over the past century. But this hasn't been a constant rise. Between 1940 and 1970, average temperatures dropped.

- Developing countries are expected to rapidly increase their carbon dioxide emissions in the next 20 years, as their populations increase and they acquire fossil fuel-burning technologies.

- Cuts in carbon dioxide and CFC emissions must be made worldwide to be effective. The U.S. and other developed countries have agreed to supply developing countries with technology and funds to help them replace CFCs.

- Most scientists agree that the increase of greenhouse gases will affect the world's climate. But they're unsure about when these changes will start (if they haven't already), how much the world will warm up or cool down, what specific regions will be affected, and how rapidly the changes will take place.

- Some experts say it will take decades of research before they can be sure if the earth's climate is warming up. Others feel that we have enough evidence now.

RANGER RICK'S NATURESCOPE: POLLUTION—PROBLEMS AND SOLUTIONS
(See *Something's in the Air*—p 36)

Setting—In front of the Environmental Protection Agency (EPA) building. The air pollutants are picketing the EPA. Some carry picket signs with phrases such as "Dirty Air—Let's Keep It That Way," "Down with the Clean Air Act," and so on. TV reporters Connie Lung and Harry Wheezer are at center stage. In turn, each pollutant comes over to be interviewed, while the other pollutants continue to picket in the background.

Connie: Hi! I'm Connie Lung.
Harry: And I'm Harry Wheezer. We're here at the Environmental Protection Agency to cover a late-breaking story. Eight of the world's worst air pollutants are picketing the EPA to protest clean air legislation.
Connie: In tonight's special report, we'll give you the scoop on where these pollutants come from and the ways they can hurt people and other living things.
Harry: Our first interview is with the Particulates.
(Particulates walk over, carrying signs and chanting.)
Particulates:
Dust, soot, and grime.
Pollution's not a crime.
Soot, grime, and dust,
The EPA's unjust!

Connie: *(coughs)* So—you're the Particulates.
Particulate 1 (Soot): Yeah—I'm Soot, this is Grime, and this is Dust.
Harry: You guys are those tiny bits of pollution that make the air look really dirty?
Grime: Yeah! Some of us are stirred up during construction, mining, and farming. *(throws some dirt in air)*
Soot: But most of us get into the air when stuff is burned—like gasoline in cars and trucks, or coal in a power plant, and even wood in a wood-burning stove!
Dust: And we just love to get into your eyes and make them itch, and make your throat hurt, and—
Grime: *(interrupts)* Come on, Dust, quit bragging! We gotta get back to the picket line.

(Particulates return to picket line. Carbon Monoxide sneaks up behind Harry.)
Harry: Let's introduce the folks at home to our next pollutant, Carbon Monoxide. Hey, where did he go? Oh, there you are! Pretty sneaky, Carbon Monoxide!
Carbon Monoxide: Yeah, sneaking up on people is what I do best. I get into the air when cars and trucks burn fuel—but you can't see or smell me.
Connie: Then how can we tell when you're around?
Carbon Monoxide: You'll find out when you breathe me in! I can give you a bad headache and make you really tired. *(gives an evil laugh)*
Harry: *(yawns)* Oh—I see what you mean. Thanks for talking with us, Monoxide. *(yawns again)*
(Carbon Monoxide returns to picket line.)
Connie: *(checking notes)* Next we'd like you to meet some of the most dangerous air pollutants—the Toxics.
(Toxics walk over, carrying signs and chanting.)
Toxics:
Benzene, xylene, toluene,
You'll find us in your gasoline.
Don't worry, we won't make you sneeze;
Instead we'll give you lung disease.

Asbestos, mercury, and even lead,
Just breathe us and you may be dead.
Poison's what we're all about.
So you better stay clear; you better watch out!

Harry: You Toxics are made up of all kinds of poisons. How do you get into the air?
Toxic 1: Hey, man, we come from just about everywhere. Chemical plants, dry cleaners, oil refineries, hazardous waste sites, paint factories . . .

Toxic 2: Yeah, and cars and trucks dump a lot of us into the air too. You probably don't know it, but gasoline is loaded with us toxics.

Toxic 3: Wow, that's for sure. There's benzene, toluene—all kinds of great stuff in gas.

Connie: Scientists say you cause cancer and other kinds of diseases. What do you think of that?

Toxic 4: They can't prove a thing!

Toxic 5: That's why we're here—to make sure you people don't pass any more laws that might keep us out of the air. C'mon, Toxics—we're outta here!

(Toxics return to picket line. Sulfur Dioxide walks over.)

Connie: Next we'd like you to meet Sulfur Dioxide. *(turns to face Sulfur Dioxide)* I understand you just blew in from the Midwest.

Sulfur: Hey, I wouldn't miss this for all the pollution in New York City!

Harry: I'm sure the folks at home would like to know how you get into our air.

Sulfur: Well, heck, don't they read the newspapers? I've been making the front page at least once a week! Most of the time, I shoot out of smokestacks when power plants burn coal to make electricity.

Connie: And what kinds of nasty things do you do?

Sulfur: Nasty—that's me! *(snickers)* I think it's cool to make it hard for some people to breathe. And I can make trees and other plants grow more slowly. But here's the *most* rotten thing I do: When I get way up into the air, I mix with water in the sky, and presto! You get acid rain! *(sprays water at audience)*

Harry: Acid rain is a big problem. It can kill fish and other animals that live in lakes and rivers, and some scientists think it makes trees sick. Acid rain can even eat away at statues and buildings.

Sulfur: *(proudly)* That's right. Hey, I can even travel a long way to do my dirty work. If I get pumped out of a smokestack in Ohio, I can ride the wind for hundreds of miles and turn up as acid rain in Vermont!

Connie: I sure hope we can get rid of you soon, Sulfur Dioxide!

Sulfur: Good luck, suckers! I gotta do some more picketing before I catch the next north wind!

(Sulfur Dioxide returns to picket line. Nitros walk over.)

Harry: *(to the audience)* He's really rotten!

Nitros: *(all together)* You think Sulfur Dioxide is rotten? You haven't met rotten until you've met us!

Connie: You must be the Nitrogen Oxides.

Nitro 1: Just call us the Nitros for short. *(turns to audience)* Give me an "N"!

Audience and other Nitros respond: "N"!

Nitro 2: Give me an "I"!

Audience/other Nitros: "I"!

Nitro 3: Give me a "T"!

Audience/other Nitros: "T"!

Nitro 4: Give me an "R"!

Audience/other Nitros: "R"!

Nitro 5: Give me an "O"!

Audience/other Nitros: "O"!

Nitro 1: What's that spell?

Audience/other Nitros: NITRO!

Nitro 2: What's that mean?

Other Nitros: DIRTY AIR!

Harry: Hey, I didn't know pollutants could spell.

Nitro 4: Very funny, Harry.

Connie: So, how do you Nitros get into the air?

Nitro 5: We get airborne when cars, planes, trucks, and power plants burn fuel.

Harry: And what happens once you're in the air?

Nitro 1: We can make people's lungs hurt when they breathe—especially people who already have asthma.

Nitro 2: And, like Sulfur Dioxide, we mix with water in the air and form acid rain.

Nitro 3: But we also make another form of pollution. And here she is—BAD OZONE!

(Bad Ozone waves and walks over. Nitros return to picket line.)

Bad Ozone: City life—I love it! The sun, the soot, the smell of car exhaust! It makes me come alive.

Connie: Exactly how do you "come alive"?

Bad Ozone: Well, when my friends, the Nitros, pour into the air, they get together with some other pollutants. As the sun shines on all these lovely pollutants, it heats them

RANGER RICK'S NATURESCOPE: POLLUTION—PROBLEMS AND SOLUTIONS
(See The Awful Eight—p 39)

up—and creates me, bad ozone. And where there's ozone, there's smog.

Harry: *(to audience)* Smog is made up mostly of ozone.

Connie: That's right, Harry. And smog can really make city life miserable. It can make your eyes burn, your head ache, and it can damage your lungs.

Harry: But what I want to know is, if ozone is so bad, why are people worried about holes in the ozone layer?

(Good Ozone walks in from offstage.)

Good Ozone: That low-level ozone is my rotten twin sister—she's just a good gas turned bad! I'm the good ozone that forms a layer high above the earth. I help absorb the harmful rays of the sun.

Bad Ozone: *(nastily to Good Ozone)* So what are you doing here, Sis?

Good Ozone: I'm here to *support* the clean air laws. If certain chemicals keep getting pumped into the atmosphere, I'll disappear. And without me, the harmful rays of the sun will kill some kinds of plants and give many more people skin cancer and eye disease!

Harry: But what kinds of chemicals are making you disappear?

Good Ozone: It's those terrible CFCs!

(CFCs walk over from picket line.)

CFC 1: Hey, we're not so bad! People have used us CFCs to make *(point to different parts of costume)* plastic foam cups, fast-food containers, packing material, coolants for refrigerators and air conditioners—all kinds of things. *(throws "peanuts" into audience)*

CFC 2: So what if we destroy a little bit of ozone? There's enough to last for years!

CFC 3: Yeah—who needs ozone anyway?

Good Ozone: People do! Tell them what *else* you CFCs are doing!

CFC 4: What's Ozone complaining about *now*—global warming? *(EPA scientists walk in from offstage. Good and Bad Ozone walk offstage.)*

Scientist 1: Excuse me, but did I just hear someone mention global warming?

CFC 2: Yeah. What do *you* want?

Scientist 2: We just happen to be experts on global climate change.

Connie: Are CFCs really changing the world's climate?

Scientist 1: Well, we're not positive. But over the past 100 years or so, we've poured gases, such as CFCs and carbon dioxide, into the air.

Scientist 2: And as they build up in the atmosphere, these gases may be acting like the glass in a greenhouse.

Scientist 1: That's right. They let the radiation from the sun in—but they keep the heat from getting out. And this may be causing the earth's climate to become warmer.

Harry: I've read that if the temperature goes up, sea levels may rise. Wow, some cities on the coast might be under water some day!

Scientist 1: It's certainly possible.

Scientist 2: Well, nice talking with you all, but we've got to do some more research so that we can really nail these pollutants. *(Points to CFCs. CFCs give scientist a dirty look, stick out tongues. Scientists walk offstage.)*

CFC 1: Hey, we're not even the biggest cause of global climate change. You gotta talk to another of the big pollutants about that.

Harry: *(checks notes)* There's only one other pollutant on the list— Carbon Dioxide.

(CFCs return to picket line. Carbon Dioxide 1 and 2 walk over.)

Dioxide 1: Did we hear you mention our name? We didn't use

to be thought of as a bad gas. About a hundred years ago, there was just the right amount of us in the air.

Dioxide 2: But then people started burning things—they built power plants that burn coal and cars and trucks that burn gasoline. And they started cutting down and burning forests! Every bit of that burning releases us into the air.

Dioxide 1: As more and more of us got into the air, people started saying that the earth was warming up—because of us!

Dioxide 2: Yeah—like it's our fault! *(to audience)* The reason you're in such a mess is because you use so much fuel and cut down so many trees!

Connie: You're right, Carbon Dioxide. Maybe we should be doing a special report on people—we're the ones who are really causing air pollution.

Harry: But people can change! *(turns to audience)* How about you? Can you think of some ways that people can help fight air pollution?

(Audience responds with ideas, such as driving cars less, using less electricity, conserving forests, planting trees, and so on.)

Connie: And that's the end of our special report. The bottom line? These air pollutants are a pretty tough bunch—but people create them, and people can get rid of them. Thank you and good night.

POLLUTANT CURTAIN CALL
THE END

Pollution Points

DAY 2—April 27
1. Winds blow radioactive cloud northwest over Gdansk, Poland.

DAY 3—April 28
2. Radioactive cloud reaches Stockholm, Sweden.
3. Radioactive cloud reaches Helsinki, Finland.
4. Radioactive cloud reaches Oslo, Norway.

DAY 4—April 29
5. Radiation continues moving north through Scandinavia and reaches Trondheim, Norway.
6. Radiation detected in Copenhagen, Denmark.
7. Winds carry radioactive cloud to Prague, Czechoslovakia.

DAY 5—April 30
8. Cloud moves over Munich, West Germany. Heavy radiation falls when it rains in this area.
9. High amounts of radioactive particles wash out when it rains in Vienna, Austria.
10. Radioactive cloud reaches Geneva, Switzerland.

DAY 6—May 1
11. Cloud travels to Rome, Italy.
12. Radioactive cloud reaches Budapest, Hungary.
13. Winds carry radioactive cloud to Zagreb, Yugoslavia.
14. Radiation detected in Paris, France.
15. Radioactive cloud reaches Tromso, Norway.

DAY 7—May 2
16. Small amounts of radiation measured near Reykjavik, Iceland.
17. Radiation reaches Bucharest, Romania.
18. Winds carry radioactive particles into Brussels, Belgium.
19. Radioactive cloud moves over London, England. High amounts of radiation wash out when it rains north of London.
20. Radioactive cloud detected in Sofia, Bulgaria.

DAY 8—May 3
21. Radioactive cloud reaches Glasgow, Scotland.
22. Winds carry radioactive cloud to Athens, Greece.
23. Radioactive particles detected in Ankara, Turkey.

DAY 9—May 4
24. Radiation reaches Beirut, Lebanon.

DAY 10—May 5
25. Radiation detected in Damascus, Syria.

DAY 11—May 6
26. Radioactive particles reach Kuwait, the capital city of Kuwait.
27. Radioactive cloud moves over Xian, China.

DAY 12—May 7
28. Radioactive particles reach Tokyo, Japan.

DAY 18—May 13
29. Slight amount of radiation detected in Richland, Washington, in the United States.

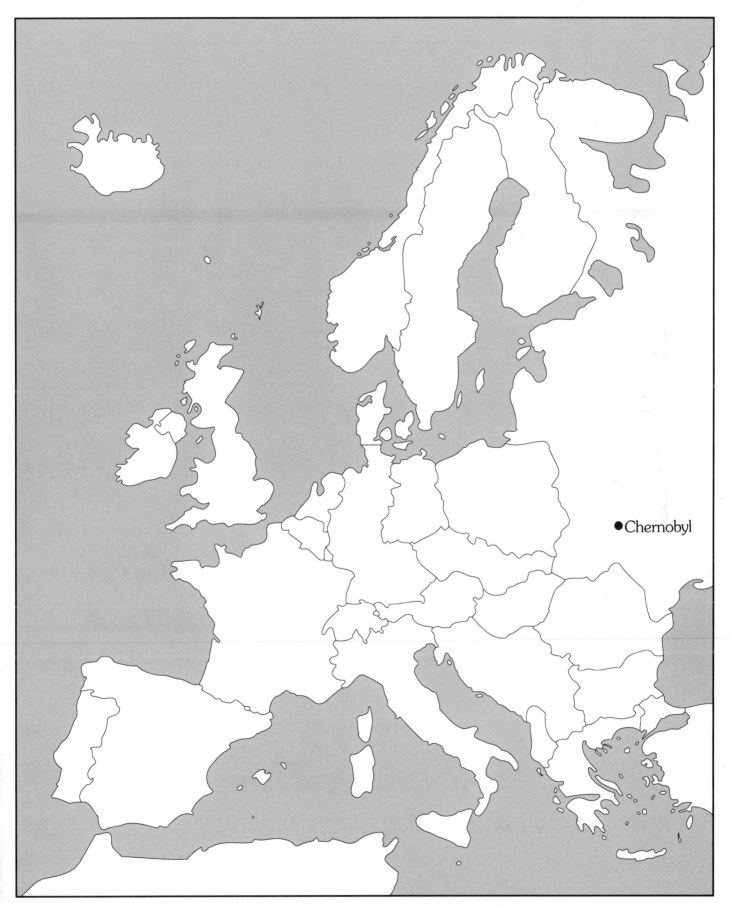

●Chernobyl

SCIENTIST 1

It's time to face the facts—the increasing amounts of carbon dioxide and CFCs in the atmosphere are making our planet's climate warm up. We've seen the warning signs in our increasing world temperatures. The 1980s were the hottest decade in recorded history—six of the warmest years ever recorded were 1981, 1983, 1986, 1987, 1988, and 1989. While this isn't proof that global warming has begun, it certainly should warn us that something is happening to our climate.

Over the past 100 years, average world temperatures have risen by about 1°F. That may not seem like much of an increase, but keep in mind that temperatures today are only about 9°F warmer than they were during the last ice age. It takes only a small change in temperature to cause big changes in our world. And if we continue to put as much carbon dioxide into the atmosphere as we're putting into it now, the world's average temperature may increase by 3 to 10°F within the next 50 years.

If temperatures do rise, we can expect some drastic changes to take place. As temperatures go up, sea levels will rise and many coastal areas will become flooded. The warming could make droughts occur more often in certain areas. Some places, like the Midwest, could become so hot and dry that many crops couldn't grow there anymore. And all over the world, plants and animals may not be able to adapt quickly enough to the sudden changes in their habitats. Some species could even become extinct.

Some people claim that we should wait until we're absolutely sure of global warming before we do anything to control it. I disagree. If we wait too long, it may be too late to prevent damage from the warming trend.

We must cut carbon dioxide production by at least 20 percent and phase out CFCs *now*. And since people in the United States produce a lot of the carbon dioxide and CFCs that go into the air, we have to set an example for the rest of the world. We must develop safer chemicals to replace CFCs. We have to switch to solar power and other alternative energy sources. And until we make that switch, we have to use less fossil fuel and become more energy efficient. Industries that continue to use coal and other fossil fuels should be taxed for the excessive carbon dioxide they release. A tax should also be placed on gasoline to encourage people to drive less. And car makers should be required by law to make cars that get better gas mileage.

Individuals must do their part too, by taking public transportation instead of driving their cars so much and by buying more energy-efficient appliances and cars. And we have to stop the burning of tropical rain forests. By preserving these forests, we can reduce carbon dioxide emissions caused by the burning *and* save the trees and other vegetation that help absorb carbon dioxide.

It will cost money to make some of these changes. But it's better to pay the price now—not later when the effects of global warming can't be reversed.

SCIENTIST 2

There's been a lot of concern lately that the world's climate is warming up. Some scientists say that the increased amounts of carbon dioxide and CFCs in the atmosphere are causing this global warming. According to them, the only way to avoid global disaster is to cut carbon dioxide emissions by at least 20 percent—a move that would affect people all over the world.

I say there's not enough scientific evidence to back up this call for drastic action. Let's consider the facts. It is true that there's more carbon dioxide in our atmosphere than there used to be and that we have added gases, such as CFCs, that were never part of our atmosphere before. But there's just not enough evidence to prove that these gases are making the world warm up. In the past 100 years, average world temperatures have risen by only 1°F. And this hasn't been a constant rise—between 1940 and 1970, world temperatures actually dropped, and some scientists suggested that another ice age might be on the way. This latest rise could be just another small change in a natural climate cycle.

It's very important to keep in mind that many of the predictions about the effects of global warming are based on *theory*. Scientists have come up with these predictions by plugging information about our atmosphere into computers. The computers make predictions about what will happen if we add certain amounts of carbon dioxide and other gases. The problem is, different computer models can give you different answers! Some models have predicted that the increase in carbon dioxide will cause more clouds to form. These clouds would block sunlight and cancel out much of the warming. And, according to other models, it's possible that the earth's huge oceans will absorb any extra heat. We just don't know enough yet about how our atmosphere works.

Because of this uncertainty about what is really happening in our atmosphere, I believe we need to do more research before we make any big changes. To significantly cut the amount of carbon dioxide we put into the atmosphere would make life harder for many people—especially those living in less developed countries. How can we ask them to cut back on releasing carbon dioxide when they're just now getting the cars and factories that people in more developed countries have had for so long? And in the United States, cutting carbon dioxide production would cost billions of dollars each year. Forcing industries to stop using fossil fuels might drive some smaller firms out of business and hurt people in regions where coal mining provides many jobs. We must do more research before we make changes that, in the end, may cause more harm than good.

QUESTIONS

1. What are the main points brought up by each scientist?

2. What are the advantages and disadvantages of the alternative presented by Scientist 1?

3. What are the advantages and disadvantages of the alternative presented by Scientist 2?

4. Can you think of a course of action that is a compromise between the two plans presented by the scientists?

5. What do you think is the best course of action? Why do you feel this is the best thing to do?

6. Do you think it's important to stay informed about scientific issues? Why or why not? What are some ways you can affect the decisions that politicians and other leaders make about the environment?

TROUBLED WATERS

W hen you bite into a juicy, spot-free apple, you probably don't think about water pollution. But there's a direct link between "perfect" apples and tainted water: Most of the apples we eat have been sprayed with pesticides to control insect damage. And these pesticides often wash into water supplies, contaminating drinking water and poisoning wildlife.

The link between water pollutants and their source isn't always obvious. But water quality experts agree that understanding what causes water pollution is the first step toward solving the pollution problems that plague our lakes, streams, rivers, oceans, and underground water supplies.

WATER POLLUTION AT THE SURFACE

Surface water is easy to see: It's the water that flows in our rivers and streams and that fills our lakes, bays, and oceans. *Groundwater,* however, is hidden from view: It fills the spaces between soil particles and rocks underground. (See page 58 for more about groundwater.)

In general, the pollutants that reach surface water come from one of two sources. *Point* pollution comes from readily identifiable sources, such as a pipe draining from an industrial plant or sewage treatment facility. This type of pollution is relatively easy to track down and control. *Nonpoint* pollution, however, cannot be traced to any one source and is much more difficult to control. Nonpoint water pollution includes *runoff,* which is all the material that washes off city streets, suburban lawns, and agricultural land, and all the air pollutants that fall into waterways.

Here's a rundown of the materials that get into surface water—from both point and nonpoint sources—and the problems they can cause.

Tiny Troublemakers: When disease-causing organisms such as bacteria and viruses get into surface water, they can spread dysentery, hepatitis, and other diseases. One of the major sources of these organisms is untreated human waste. In most areas of the U.S., water carrying human waste passes through sewage treatment plants before being released into surface water. Sewage treatment plants treat wastewater to kill disease-causing bacteria and viruses. But during heavy storms, the wastewater coming into the plants may back up and overflow directly into surface water without being treated. Untreated waste can also wash directly into surface water if a treatment plant isn't working properly. (In some parts of the U.S., wastewater is treated by septic systems instead of sewage treatment plants. And many of these septic systems can cause groundwater pollution. See page 58.)

Oxygen Hogs: Untreated human waste can do more than transmit diseases; it can also rob water of oxygen. And other biodegradable waste that gets into surface water, such as animal and food waste, can have the same effect. That's because this waste is broken down in the water by bacteria and other organisms that use oxygen to do their "work." And these organisms may use so much of the oxygen in the water that fish and other aquatic organisms can't survive.

Malfunctioning or overloaded sewage treatment plants are one source of biodegradable waste. Another is runoff. Tremendous amounts of animal waste wash into surface water from feedlots and other agricultural land each year. And runoff from yards and streets often carries yard and pet waste.

Green Growth: When nitrate-containing fertilizers and phosphate-containing detergents get into surface water, they can deplete oxygen supplies, just as biodegrad-

able waste can. The nitrates and phosphates in these products act as fertilizer for algae and can cause them to grow at a tremendous rate, creating huge algal "blooms." As the algae grow, die, and decompose, they use a lot of the oxygen in the water. Nitrates and phosphates can also cause other problems. For example, nitrates can end up in drinking water and make the water unfit to drink.

Chemical Cornucopia: There are more than 65,000 commercially available chemicals in the U.S. These chemicals are ingredients in many products we use every day and are also used in many industrial processes. Unfortunately many of them also end up polluting our water.

Some of these chemicals are dumped directly into water. For example, each year industries legally dump more than 500 million pounds of toxic chemicals directly into surface water. But a lot of chemicals get into surface water inadvertently. For instance, runoff carries tons of pesticides, heavy metals, and other chemicals into surface water each year.

Chemicals that get into surface water can poison fish and other animals outright. They can also accumulate to toxic levels in the tissues of animals. And they can accumulate in bottom sediments, forming reservoirs of chemicals that can continue to affect aquatic life for years.

Poisons from the Sky: In parts of the Northeast and in other areas, lakes once teeming with fish, aquatic insects, and many other species are now almost devoid of life. The culprit? Acid rain.

Acid rain can kill aquatic life in several ways. For example, so much acid rain may fall in an area that the pH of surface water drops. Since many aquatic species are adapted to living only within a certain pH range, the change in pH may be enough to kill them or prevent them from reproducing. (For more about pH and acid rain, see "Acid Tests" on page 42.)

Acids, however, are not the only compounds reaching surface water from the air. PCBs, DDT, and other airborne toxics, some of them carried in the atmosphere for thousands of miles, also end up in surface water. These compounds may kill animals directly, build up in their tissues, or cause disease. And when people and other animals eat aquatic creatures contaminated with these chemicals, they may develop serious illnesses.

A Dirty Problem: When rain runs off land that's been disturbed by bulldozers, logging trucks, and other equipment, it picks up dirt and silt and carries them into surface water. Dredging operations also dump a lot of sediment into surface water. Once in the water, sediment can keep sunlight from reaching aquatic plants, can clog fish gills, and can smother bottom-dwelling organisms.

Oily Messes: Any time a tanker runs aground and spills millions of gallons of oil into the sea, the event makes world headlines. But the amount of oil spilled in accidents like this represents only a fraction of the total amount of oil that contaminates our water resources each year. For example, tankers routinely dump oil into the oceans when they clean out their tanks, refineries pump oil-laced wastewater into surface water, and oil from city streets washes into surface water.

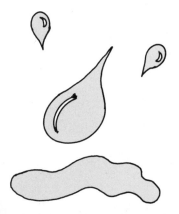

Oil's effects on wildlife can be devastating. Some animals, including birds, mammals, and fish, may be killed by ingesting the oil. Many others may die from eating contaminated prey or by getting their feathers or fur coated with oil, which causes them to lose their ability to stay warm. *(continued next page)*

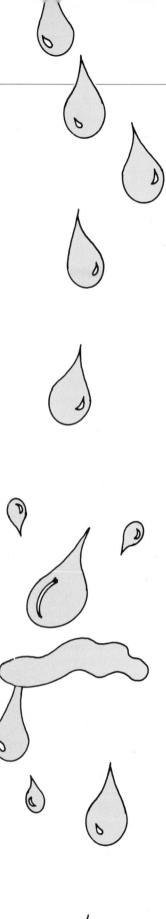

GROUNDWATER: THE HIDDEN RESOURCE

Approximately half of the people living in the U.S. rely on groundwater for their drinking water. Groundwater is also one of the most important sources of irrigation water. Unfortunately some of the groundwater in every state has become tainted with pollutants. And some scientists fear that the percentage of contaminated groundwater may increase as toxic chemicals dumped on the ground during the past several decades slowly make their way into groundwater supplies.

So What Is Groundwater? Many people picture groundwater as underground rivers or lakes. But, as we mentioned earlier, it's actually water that fills the spaces between rocks and soil particles underground—in much the same way as water fills a sponge. Most groundwater is precipitation that has soaked into the ground. And groundwater sometimes feeds lakes, springs, and other surface water.

A Seeping Problem: Pollutants that contaminate groundwater seep into it through the ground. And the pollutants themselves are many of the same compounds that contaminate surface water. For example, pesticides and fertilizers often seep into groundwater supplies. Road salt, toxic substances from mining sites, and used motor oil may all end up in groundwater too. Untreated waste may leak into groundwater from faulty septic tanks. And toxic chemicals may leach out of landfills or leak from underground storage wells and seep into groundwater. Unlike tainted surface water, contaminated groundwater can be almost impossible to clean up.

The Health Impact: Contaminated groundwater can have serious health effects. For instance, people whose drinking water has become contaminated by septic tank waste may contract hepatitis, dysentery, or other diseases. People may also be poisoned by toxics that have seeped into their well water. And if they drink water contaminated with certain chemicals over a long enough period of time, they may develop liver and kidney problems, cancer, or other serious illnesses. Contaminated groundwater can also harm wildlife if it gets into surface water.

PROTECTION AND PREVENTION

Finding answers to our water pollution problems won't be easy. For one thing, in addition to the pollutants we've already mentioned, there are others getting into our water that we must deal with too, such as radioactive waste, heated industrial wastewater, and trash. There are also many stumbling blocks in the way. For example, cleanup of toxic waste dump sites that could be or are polluting groundwater is progressing slowly because of legal battles over responsibility and high cleanup costs. And many of the laws designed to protect our water resources are not being enforced. But because water is such a vital part of our lives, there's too much at stake *not* to deal with the problems.

New Technologies: One thing people are working on is the development of new methods of treating wastewater. For example, people-made wetlands and other systems that are often cheaper and cleaner than traditional treatment plants are being used in some communities to treat sewage. People are also trying to find new ways to remove toxics from water and from bottom sediments.

An Ounce of Prevention: Cleaning up polluted water can be extremely expensive. So keeping pollutants out of our water in the first place is the best way to ensure that we have clean water. Many individuals and industries around the country are taking steps to do just that. For example, some industries are reducing their production of toxic chemicals and developing ways to make their products without using toxic raw materials. And many people have switched to phosphate-free detergents and other less-polluting products. In addition, governments are passing tough water pollution control measures designed to prevent water pollution. (See page 83 for information about legislation designed to protect water.)

Away with Waste!

Listen to a rhyming story to find out about sources of water pollution.

Objectives:
Describe some of the ways people pollute waterways. Describe some of the effects of water pollution.

Ages:
Primary and Intermediate

Materials:
* story on page 60
* drawing paper
* crayons or markers
* construction paper (optional)
* stapler (optional)
* glue (optional)
* copies of page 60 (optional)

Subjects:
Science, Language Arts, and Art

By listening to a rhyming story about water pollution in one community, your kids can discover how pollution can affect waterways. They'll also discover that the waste we wash "away" can have harmful effects later on.

Before reading the story, ask the kids to name some of the ways they use water. (for drinking, bathing, brushing teeth, cleaning clothes and dishes, and so on) Then ask them what happens to the water that drains out of their washing machines and dishwashers or washes down their sinks. (Don't worry whether the kids know the answer at this point. You'll be discussing what happens to household water with them after they hear the story.) Explain that many people never think about what happens to the water they use in their households each day. They also don't think about what happens to the water that runs off their streets and yards.

Now tell the kids you're going to read them a story about a town called "Away" and about how people in the town polluted the water in a nearby bay without realizing what was happening. Tell the kids to listen carefully to the story to find out just how the water in the bay became polluted. Also tell them to listen for the word "away." Each time they hear it they should make a "hitch-hiking" motion over their shoulder with their thumb to represent something going away.

After you read the story, discuss it with the kids. Ask them if waste from Away simply disappeared. (no) What happened to the waste? (it ended up in the bay) Then go over the verses in the first half of the story to be sure the kids understood what was happening in each one. Use the information under "Where Did It Go?" below to help with the discussion.

Afterward pass out crayons or markers and drawing paper and have the kids draw pictures of the story. They might draw the people in the town, the bay when it was polluted, or the bay when it was cleaned up again. If you're working with older kids, you might want to have them create their own picture books of the story. Pass out copies of page 60 and have the kids draw a picture to go along with each verse of the story. Then have them glue their pictures on sheets of construction paper, copy the words of each verse onto the pages, and staple the pages together.

(continued next page)

WHERE DID IT GO?

Down the Drain: When most people in the U.S. rinse something down their drain, flush their toilet, or do a load of wash, the wastewater goes to sewage treatment plants to be purified. These plants remove dirt, biodegradable material such as food waste, and many other pollutants from the water before the water is dumped into waterways. They also treat the water to kill harmful bacteria and viruses. But most plants can't remove all the chemical pollutants. For example, chemicals that are used in paint thinners and phosphates that are used in many detergents pass right through some sewage treatment plants.

Off the Streets: Oil, dirt, litter, and anything else that's on the streets washes into storm drains. In most areas of the country, these drains empty into a series of underground pipes that eventually dump directly into waterways.

Industrial Pollution: Factories that make chemicals, paper, medicines, steel, and many other products can create a lot of pollutants. At one time, industries could legally dump waste into waterways. But pollution-control laws now limit the materials that industries can dump into surface water. These controls have greatly reduced water pollution. However, not all the types of industrial waste are regulated. In addition, some experts feel that some of the regulations are not strict enough to protect aquatic systems.

Trashing the Water: When trash gets thrown overboard it can create an ugly mess—both in the water and on shore after it's washed up. Trash can also harm or even kill wildlife. For example, thousands of sea birds and marine mammals die each year after eating or becoming entangled in plastic debris floating in the ocean.

This is the tale of a town called **Away**—
A town that was built on the shore of a bay.
A town where the folks didn't think much about
What they dumped in their water day in and day out.

For one thing, a sink was an excellent place
To get rid of messes and not leave a trace.
Cleansers and cleaners and yesterday's lunch
Went **away** down the drain with a gurgly crunch.

At everyone's house there was laundry to do.
Day after day, how those laundry piles grew!
Load after load was washed, rinsed, and spun
And **away** went the water when each load was done.

On Main Street each day there were sidewalks to sweep.
The litter and dirt were swept into the street.
And then when it rained, everything washed **away**
Into drains in the roads that dumped into the bay.

A mill there made "stuff" for the townfolks to use,
But a pipe from the mill churned out oodles of ooze.
And the ooze, well it goozed from the pipe to the bay
Where it bubbled and glubbed as it drifted **away**.

When the weather was warm, it was always a treat
To sail on the bay and bring picnics to eat.
But when folks were finished, they'd toss all their trash
Overboard and **away** with a plop and a splash.

Then folks started seeing that things weren't quite right;
The bay had become an unbearable sight.
Beaches were covered with garbage and glop
That rolled in with the waves—and the waves didn't
 stop.

The fish in the bay all seemed sluggish and sick,
The algae was everywhere—slimy and thick.
The birds near **Away** were all suffering too,
'Cause the fish they were eating were covered with goo.

So a meeting was called to discuss the sick bay
And townspeople came from all parts of **Away**.
And during the meeting one person proclaimed,
"I know who's at fault: We *all* should be blamed."

"For years we've washed chemicals, dirt, and debris
Down our sinks, off our streets, and out pipes—
 so you see,
Although we all thought that our waste went **away**,
It all ended up going into the bay."

"Now the bay is a mess—full of trash, soap, and goop,
The water's turned green—like a bowl of pea soup.
And our wildlife is sick from the garbage and grime;
The bay needs our help, right now while there's time."

The folks were all silent—they knew it was true.
And they realized now what they all had to do.
It was time to get busy—the bay couldn't wait.
If they didn't act now, it might soon be too late.

So they signed an agreement that very same minute
To care for the bay and to stop putting in it
The stuff that had made the bay icky and ill,
Like soaps that pollute and the ooze from the mill.

They also agreed to stop dumping their trash
Overboard and **away** with a plop and a splash.
And all of their efforts have been a success:
Today the bay's clean and no longer a mess.

And that is the tale of the town called **Away**—
A town where the people, to this very day,
Remember a saying that's simple and plain:
Nothing just goes **away** when it's washed down the
drain.

Guilty or Innocent?

Use clues to figure out if five people in a town are guilty of polluting water.

Objectives:
Describe several ways people pollute water. Explain some ways people can help prevent water pollution.

Ages:
Intermediate and Advanced

Materials:
* *copies of pages 66 and 67*
* *chalkboard or easel paper*

Subjects:
Science and Language Arts

I t's easy to understand that a crippled tanker leaking millions of gallons of crude oil into the ocean is polluting the water. But recognizing other forms of water pollution can be more difficult. In this activity the kids in your group will discover some of the not-so-obvious ways people can pollute water every day without realizing it.

Begin the activity by asking the kids to name some ways water gets polluted. Write their ideas on a chalkboard or piece of easel paper and tell the kids they'll be adding to the list later. Next explain the terms *groundwater* and *surface water* to the kids, using the background information on pages 56 and 58. Then pass out copies of page 67 and explain that each of the facts on the page has something to do with water pollution. Have the kids read the page, and then go over any facts they didn't understand.

Next pass out copies of page 66. The kids will see that the page has a picture and short description of five different people. The kids should read each description and then use the facts on page 67 to decide whether the person is more likely to be guilty or innocent of polluting water. Tell the kids

they should write "guilty" or "innocent" on the line following each character's description. Then, on the back of page 66, have them write a short explanation of why they think each person is guilty or innocent. Tell them to include the numbers of the facts they used to reach their answer.

When everyone has finished go over page 66 with the kids, using the answers on page 62 and the information under "Pollution Particulars." Be sure to explain that some of the actions of the people on the page might not affect overall water quality very much by themselves. But if a lot of people in the area were doing the same things, the cumulative effect could be disastrous. And this is exactly what happens in many communities throughout the U.S.

Next discuss with the kids the fact that, like the characters in the story, all of us are "guilty" of polluting water without knowing it. Every time we flush our toilets, wash our clothes, take showers, and do any number of other things that require using water, we contribute to water pollution problems. Then ask the kids if they'd like to add anything to their list of ways water gets polluted.

Afterward point out that there is a lot people can do to reduce the amount of water pollution they create. Ask the kids what kinds of things the characters on page 66 might do to reduce their effect on water quality. (Joe—use fewer and less-toxic pesticides, use natural insect predators to help control pest insects, make sure cows graze away from the stream. Leila—use collecting pans to catch liquids emptying from car; take used motor oil and antifreeze to a collection center for recycling or to a hazardous waste collection center; soak up any spilled liquids with cat litter and then take the litter to a hazardous waste collection center. Michi—switch to non-toxic lawn care. Martha—periodically check the underground storage tank for leaks; upgrade tank so it won't corrode. Sabina—use detergents that don't contain phosphates.)

(continued next page)

POLLUTION PARTICULARS

Ruinous Runoff: Anything that's sprayed, dumped, or spilled on the ground may end up in waterways. Pesticides, chemical fertilizers, animal waste, and other compounds may flow directly into waterways or wash down storm drains, which usually empty into surface water. (In many cities in the U.S., storm drains don't empty directly into waterways. Instead, material that washes into them combines with wastewater from homes and businesses and flows to a sewage treatment plant to be purified. During heavy storms, the wastewater can back up and overflow directly into surface water without being treated.) Many of the materials that get sprayed, dumped, or spilled on the ground can also soak into the soil and contaminate groundwater.

Car Care: A car engine may hold 4 to 6 quarts of oil. When this oil gets dumped down a storm drain, it can end up in a nearby waterway and create a slick that covers a huge area. Just a single quart of motor oil can contaminate up to 2 million gallons of drinking water. Other car products, including antifreeze, are also toxic and may poison aquatic animals if they get into waterways.

Storage Problems: There are approximately 5 million underground storage tanks in the U.S. and more than 200,000 of them may be leaking. These tanks are used to store gasoline, oil, chemical waste, and other hazardous liquids. Most of the tanks are made of steel, which can corrode, and they often develop leaks after about 20 years. Leaks in underground tanks and the pipes that lead to them are one of the most common sources of groundwater pollution.

Wash It All Away: The stuff that most people in the U.S. wash down their drains and flush down their toilets goes to a sewage treatment plant before it's released into rivers or other waterways. These plants can remove many of the pollutants in wastewater, including food and other organic waste. Some can even remove most of the phosphates in wastewater, but many cannot. Because of the problems they can cause, phosphates have been banned from use in detergents in some states. And equipment that can remove phosphates from wastewater is being installed in many sewage treatment plants. (See pages 56-57 for more about the problems phosphates can cause.)

Here's a way to help your group learn about one of the serious water pollution problems wildlife is up against: *bioaccumulation*. Bioaccumulation occurs when toxic substances accumulate in higher and higher concentrations from one level of a food chain to the next.

Before you get started, copy the diagram in the margin onto a large sheet of easel paper and hang it where all the kids can see it. Also gather several markers that are the same color.

Begin by telling the kids that the diagram is a simplified drawing of a food chain in a stream. Explain that the ovals at the bottom of the diagram represent freshwater mussels. (Mussels are shellfish related to clams and scallops.) Mussels get their food by filtering it from the water.

Next point out the small fish shapes and explain that they represent sculpins, a kind of fish that feeds on mussels. The sculpins, in turn, often become food for bass, represented by the large fish shape. Then tell the kids they're going to see how chemicals can affect the members of this food chain.

Divide the group into mussel and sculpin teams. (You'll need 18 children to be mussels and 6 to be sculpins.) Also assign one person to be the bass. Explain that as mussels feed they can take in pollutants—including chemicals—that are in the water. The mussels can't break down or get rid of certain chemicals, such as DDT or PCBs; instead they store the chemicals in their bodies.

Tell the kids to imagine that some PCB has gotten into the water. Each mussel in the diagram has picked up a small amount of the toxic chemical and incorporated it into its body. Have each "mussel kid" come up and use a colored marker to draw and color in a small circle on one of the mussels in the diagram. Each circle represents a small amount of PCB. (Make sure all the kids use markers that are the same color.)

Now point to the sculpins on the diagram and ask the kids what they think will happen to a sculpin that eats a mussel tainted with PCB. (Like the mussels, sculpins can't break down or excrete PCBs, and the chemical becomes part of the sculpins' bodies.) Then ask the "sculpin kids" how much PCB each sculpin will take in when it eats the mussels shown in the diagram. (three circles of PCB) Have each "sculpin kid" come up and draw three circles in the body of a sculpin.

Finally, point to the bass on the diagram and ask the kids what will happen to the PCBs after the bass eats the contaminated sculpins. (The PCBs will become part of the bass's body.) Have the person representing the bass come up and draw circles to represent how much PCB the bass will take in when it eats the six sculpins. (eighteen circles)

Afterward have the kids look at the diagram. Ask them what happened to the amount of PCB as the chemical went from one level of the food chain to the next. (It became more concentrated as it moved up the food chain.) What would they expect to happen to the level of PCB in a larger fish that ate several contaminated bass? (The concentration would be even higher in the larger fish than in the bass.) Finally, explain to the kids that in streams, lakes, bays, and other surface water, animals near the top of the food chain may have higher concentrations of toxics in their bodies than animals near the bottom of the food chain, such as plant eaters and filter feeders. Have the kids use the diagram to explain why this is so.

Note: This is a simplified representation of the process of bioaccumulation. In a real stream, the concentrations of toxics would vary from creature to creature.

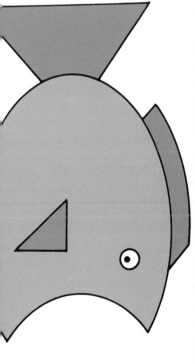

Go with the Flow

Study a watershed, and then map your local watershed.

Objectives:
Define watershed.
Explain how pollutants can affect water quality in a watershed.

Ages:
Advanced

Materials:
* *copies of page 68*
* *markers or colored pencils*
* *state highway, regional, or topographic maps*
* *tracing paper*
* *masking tape*

Subject:
Science

No matter where you live, you live within a watershed. Conditions within that watershed greatly affect the quality of the rivers and streams flowing through it. After learning about watersheds, the kids in your group will have a better understanding of how water can become polluted. But before you do this activity, make sure the kids are familiar with some of the different kinds of water pollution. You might want to do "Guilty or Innocent?" on page 61 with the kids to introduce them to some forms of water pollution.

PART 1: UPSTREAM, DOWNSTREAM

Begin by asking the kids if they've ever seen splotches of oil in a parking lot or driveway. Then tell them that by doing this activity they'll find out what eventually happens to this oil.

Next introduce the group to the term *watershed*. Using the diagram in the margin on the next page, explain that a watershed is an area of land from which rainwater and snowmelt drain into a particular stream or river. Watersheds may be small areas of land that drain water into small streams or huge areas of land that drain water into large rivers. And within each large watershed there are many smaller watersheds. A watershed is usually named after the stream or river it drains into.

Point out that as rain and snowmelt flow across land and into waterways, they wash over everything in their path: golf courses, roads, fields, lawns, woodlands, and so on. And they pick up and carry material along the way: trash, dirt, pesticides, oil, and so on.

Next pass out copies of page 68 to the group. Tell the kids to use the map at the top of the page to answer the questions on the bottom of the sheet. (If the kids are having trouble determining the boundaries of the watershed, have them look at the streams on the map to see which way they flow. Those flowing into the Cedar River are in the Cedar River watershed. See diagram on the next page.) Afterward go over the page with the kids, using the answers on the next page.

PART 2: LOCAL WATERS

USDA—Soil Conservation Service

Now have the kids map the watershed they live in. Pass out state highway, regional, or topographic maps of your area that show a stream or river flowing through (or near) your community. (For topographic maps of your area contact the U.S. Geological Survey, Map Sales, Box 25286, Denver, CO 80225.) Also pass out sheets of tracing paper, masking tape, and colored pencils or markers and tell the kids to follow these directions:

1. Find your community and the nearest stream or river on the map. Then tape tracing paper over that section of the map. (*Note:* As we discussed in the answers to Part 1, slope is the factor that separates one watershed from another. Depending on the slope of the land in your area, the watershed of the *nearest* stream or river may or may not include your community. The only way to tell is to look at slope on a

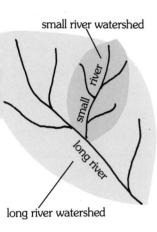

small river watershed

small river

long river

long river watershed

contour map. For this activity, the kids can assume that your community is in the watershed of the nearest stream.)

2. Use a colored pencil or marker to trace the stream or river downstream until it joins a larger river. Use the same colored pencil or marker to trace the stream upstream as far as you can and to trace all the tributaries that dump into the river or stream all along its length.

3. Use a different colored pencil or marker to trace other streams and rivers in your area.

4. Outline the watershed you live in. (Remind the kids that the watershed they live in is made up of all the land that drains into the nearest stream or river. So, to outline the watershed, they should be outlining the land surrounding the nearest waterway and all its tributaries.)

Afterward discuss the following questions as a group. (See the background information on pages 56-58 for more about the effects of particular water pollutants.)

• What types of things do rainwater and snowmelt flow over in your area? (rooftops, sidewalks, roads, agricultural land, lawns, golf courses, and so on)

• What kinds of pollutants might rainwater or snowmelt pick up as they flow through your area? (Rainwater and snowmelt that run over streets, parking lots, fertilized yards, construction sites, and so on, often pick up toxic chemicals, silt, and other pollutants. The water then flows into storm drains that empty into rivers. And water running off agricultural land often contains high amounts of animal waste, pesticides, fertilizers, dirt, and other pollutants.)

• In what other ways might your community affect water quality? (some industries dump pollutants directly into rivers; pollutants from overflowing sewage treatment facilities may wash directly into waterways; pollutants from landfills or dumps may leach into water supplies; and so on)

• Which nearby communities might be affected if your community dumped untreated sewage into the nearest stream or river? (those downstream) Which communties could affect water quality in your community? (those upstream)

Finally, ask the kids what happens to the oil splotches you talked about in the beginning of the activity. (the oil may wash into your local stream or river and be carried downstream)

(This activity was adapted from *Conserving America, Rivers Resource Guide,* © 1988 by the National Wildlife Federation and WQED/Pittsburgh.)

ANSWERS

1—see diagram below

2—Ames River watershed, Clark and New

3—Columbus, Camden, and Fairfield because they are downstream from Decker

4—Cedar River, then into Ames River; Clark River, then into Ames River. Because Sutton is closest to the Cedar River and Clarksville is closest to the Clark River. However, they could be in the same watershed, depending on the slope of the land. For example, if a mountain or hill separated Clarksville from the nearby stream, wastewater from Clarksville could flow into the Cedar River watershed. It's more likely though, that Sutton is part of the Cedar River watershed and Clarksville is part of the Clark River watershed. (*Note:* They are both in the same larger Ames River watershed.)

5—Many of the pollutants carried by the Ames and the two other rivers—pollutants that were collected from large areas of land—would end up in Lake Churchill; as pollutants accumulate in Lake Churchill, water quality could decrease significantly and aquatic plants and animals could be affected.

Explain that as rivers empty into bays, lakes, and other bodies of water, some of the waste they're carrying can accumulate in these areas. This accumulation can create big pollution problems. For example, the Chesapeake Bay and the Great Lakes are suffering from the accumulation of pollutants flowing into them.

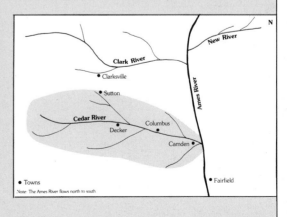

• Towns

Note: The Ames River flows north to south

Two days ago, the Granville water inspector discovered pollutants in Davies Creek, the creek that runs through the middle of town. A short time later she found contaminants in several private wells. Using the clues on page 67, can you figure out which of these Granville residents might have contributed to the problem?

JOE RAMOS

Joe Ramos's farm is one of the biggest in the Granville area. And in the summer people come from all over to buy fruits and vegetables from Joe's produce stand. Everyone knows that Joe has some of the most beautiful produce around—it's almost always free of insect damage. And when kids come to the stand with their parents, they get a special treat: a chance to see Joe's cows with their calves in the field next to Davies Creek.

LEILA KHALIL

Leila Khalil is a senior at Granville High School. A year ago she bought a car with money she'd saved from her part-time job, and since then she's learned to do most of the car's maintenance work herself. She changes her own oil, maintains the wiper fluid, and changes the antifreeze. After Leila works on her car she cleans up, pouring her used motor oil down the storm drain and hosing down her parents' driveway.

MICHI AKIZAWA

When he started his lawn-care company five years ago, Michi Akizawa had no idea it would be so successful. In a recent interview about his company, Michi said he was sure his success was due to his special training programs, in which he teaches his workers how best to apply fertilizers and weed killers. Mr. Akizawa also said he's proudest of the thick, green grass that grows on the Granville Golf Course, which his company takes care of.

MARTHA STONE

Martha Stone's small gas station near the center of town has become a landmark in Granville. Every day Martha is there selling gas, penny candy, and ice-cold sodas. And anyone who goes into the station is sure to get an earful of stories about what life in Granville used to be like. First-time visitors to the station almost always get a tour of it, starting on the sidewalk above the underground storage tank. Here Martha shows people where she carved her initials and the year "1953" in the wet cement the day before the station opened.

SABINA KAROWSKI

Sabina Karowski is a full-time homemaker with three children. On weekends, Sabina watches her kids play football, basketball, or baseball, depending on the time of year. Between games she spends a lot of time washing dirty uniforms! In fact, the clerk at the supermarket often teases Sabina about the huge boxes of heavy-duty laundry detergent she buys.

(See Guilty or Innocent?—p 61)

1. Rain and snowmelt that wash off the land may flow directly into streams, lakes, and other waterways. Or they may flow into storm drains, which, in most communities in the United States, connect to pipes that empty into waterways.

2. In most areas of the country, whatever goes down people's toilets and drains travels to a sewage treatment plant.

3. Gas stations store gasoline in underground tanks.

4. Thick, green lawns often get that way by being treated with chemical fertilizers and pesticides.

5. Sewage treatment plants treat wastewater to remove many of the pollutants in it, such as disease-causing organisms and food waste. Then they dump the treated water into rivers, streams, and other waterways.

6. Most sewage treatment plants can't remove all of the phosphates that are in wastewater.

7. Gasoline storage tanks often develop leaks after about 20 years.

8. To repair or replace a leaking gasoline storage tank, someone must dig up the tank.

9. Fertilizers, road salt, animal waste, car fluids, and other materials that wash into waterways can poison aquatic plants and animals, decrease the amount of oxygen in the water, or create other problems.

10. When substances soak through the soil, they can contaminate groundwater.

11. Many powdered laundry soaps in the United States contain some phosphates.

12. Crops grown with a lot of pesticides often look "perfect."

13. Phosphates and other chemicals that end up in waterways can cause problems for aquatic organisms.

14. Pesticides that are used to kill insects and other pests can wash into waterways and poison fish and other creatures.

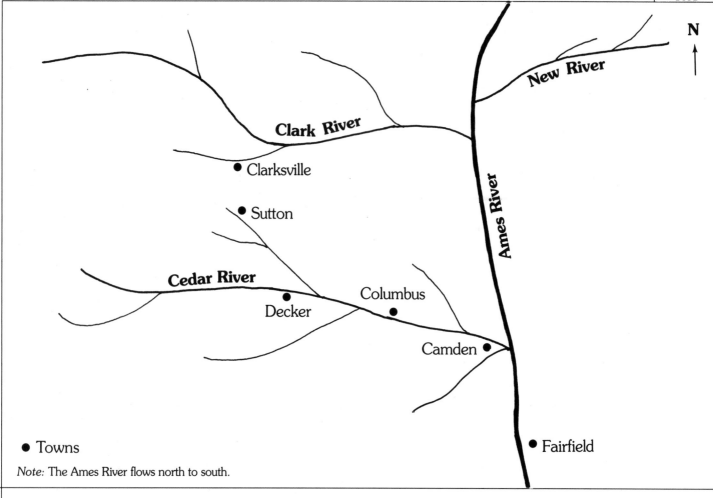

N ↑

New River

Clark River

• Clarksville

• Sutton

Ames River

Cedar River

Columbus

• Decker

• Camden

• Fairfield

• Towns

Note: The Ames River flows north to south.

1. Find the Cedar River and all the Cedar's *tributaries*—the smaller streams and rivers that flow into it. Then outline the Cedar River watershed.

2. What larger watershed is the Cedar River watershed a part of? What other rivers are part of this watershed?

3. There's a chemical manufacturing plant in Decker that dumps its waste into the Cedar River. What communities might be affected by this waste? Explain your answer.

4. Which river would animal waste and other pollutants from farms near Sutton wash into? What about from farms near Clarksville? Why would you think that Sutton and Clarksville are in two different watersheds? Is it possible for Sutton and Clarksville to be in the same watershed? Explain your answer.

5. Eventually the Ames River empties into Lake Churchill. Two other large rivers also empty into Lake Churchill. What effect might these three rivers have on conditions in the lake?

CHOICES AND CHALLENGES

Most people don't need to be convinced anymore that pollution is a serious problem. Our understanding of the causes and effects of pollution is increasing daily—and people all around the world are starting to recognize some fundamental realities about the earth and our relationship to it.

For one thing, we're starting to truly understand that the earth's resources are limited. And for another, we're becoming increasingly aware of the fact that the things we do today can have negative effects—sometimes even on a global scale—that we'll have to deal with later.

WHERE THE ACTION IS

Another realization—maybe the most important one of all—is also starting to take hold. That's the idea that everyone, from individuals to businesses to governments, has a role to play in finding solutions to pollution and other environmental problems.

Taking the Bull by the Horns: On an individual level, taking personal responsibility may mean anything from choosing consumer products that aren't overpackaged to recycling in the home to launching a campaign aimed at getting companies to behave in a more environmentally sensitive manner. The fact that these actions are effective and that people are ready and willing to put them into practice are messages that have been coming through loud and clear lately. Newspaper articles and TV programs tell of kids who've gotten their school cafeterias to stop using plastic foam lunch trays, farmers who are voluntarily shifting away from chemical pesticides, and customers who've changed company policies by questioning the wisdom of "standard operating procedures." (One woman, who watched a refrigerator repairman release ozone-damaging CFC gas out her kitchen window, was able to help convince the repair company to set up a CFC-recycling policy.)

Picking Out the Path: It makes good business sense to listen to consumers. And as more people speak up, more businesses are listening.

Many companies, seeing change as inevitable, are taking the initiative to develop environmentally sensitive practices themselves instead of waiting for regulations to force them into it. For example, some plastic manufacturers and consumer products companies are setting up plastic recycling programs. Users of CFCs—including corporations as diverse as phone companies and auto manufacturers—are searching for CFC substitutes or investing in CFC-recycling equipment. And one northeastern utility company is participating in a model program: Responding to concern about the possibility of global warming, the utility has agreed to pay for a project to plant 52 million trees. Theoretically, the new trees will absorb about the same amount of carbon dioxide that one of the utility's new power plants is expected to generate.

Government Involvement: The business world isn't the only sector that's responding to the growing concern about pollution and other environmental problems. So are governments. At the local level, communities all across the nation are setting up recycling programs. And some recycling programs that have already been in place for a while are being expanded to include not just newspapers, aluminum cans, and glass, but also plastic, tin, cardboard, yard waste, and other recyclables.

State environmental agendas are getting stronger and more comprehensive too, with dozens of state legislatures addressing everything from solid waste disposal to global climate change and ozone depletion. Several states are considering a ban on disposable diapers, plastic food packaging that can't be recycled, and other throwaways, and laws are on the books in New Jersey, Vermont, and other states to cut down on carbon dioxide emissions. And on a national level, laws continue to be passed to combat pollution. (See page 83 for a rundown of some of the most important anti-pollution laws.)

A Global Agreement: One of the most significant environmental agreements ever attempted is an international treaty to protect the ozone layer. First drafted in 1987 and currently backed by nearly 100 nations, the treaty, called the Montreal Protocol, calls for an international phase-out of CFCs. The original treaty specified a 50-percent reduction in these ozone-destroying chemicals by the turn of the century, but recent evidence concerning the rates of atmospheric ozone thinning has prompted a revised agreement that calls instead for a complete phase-out of CFCs by the same time. Part of the CFC phase-out plan calls for developed nations to help less developed nations cut down on or forego the development of CFC- technology by giving them financial and technological assistance to find and use alternatives.

FORWARD TO THE FUTURE

Multinational environmental agreements, increasing corporate sensitivity to pollution and other environmental concerns, and a heightened understanding of how each of us affects the world all point to a shift in how we view our relationship with the planet. And this shift may be signaling the rise of a worldwide movement that considers the protection of the environment to be one of the highest priorities.

Taking the Environment Seriously: Statements from world leaders seem to support this idea. In a speech to the United Nations General Assembly, Soviet President Mikhail Gorbachev linked the health of the environment to international economic security which, he stated, is "inconceivable unless related not only to disarmament but also to the elimination of the threat to the world's environment." And in a special document addressing the environment, Pope John Paul II encouraged the United Nations to include "the right to a safe environment" in its Universal Declaration of Human Rights.

Building a Sustainable Society: A concern for environmental quality shared by individuals, businesses, and world leaders and governments is the first step toward creating a more *sustainable* society. Using the planet's resources in a sustainable way would mean that our activities wouldn't seriously pollute, destroy, or permanently damage the resources on which we depend. (Sustainable agricultural practices, for example, don't pollute the soil with pesticide residue.) Keeping the long-term effects of human activities in mind would be the basis of a sustainable society—and such an approach to the earth and its resources could go a long way toward solving current pollution problems and preventing new ones.

A Long-Term View: Of course, a sustainable approach to living on the planet has always been a part of some cultures. But what's needed now is a worldwide focus on the long-term effects of human activities on land, water, and air. This will definitely mean that, in the future, individuals, businesses, and governments will have to do things a lot differently than we've been doing them. But there's no reason to think we won't be able to overcome the environmental problems we're facing. Gro Harlem Brundtland, former prime minister of Norway, takes a positive approach to the environmental challenges that lie ahead of us. "I have a basic belief," she has said, "that what is wise is possible to do."

Pollution Solutions

Make a flip-up page that shows solutions to common pollution problems.

Objective:
Describe some ways to help solve pollution problems.

Ages:
Primary

Materials:
- copies of pages 79 and 80
- crayons or markers
- glue
- scissors

Subjects:
Science and Social Studies

Young kids, like everyone else, can do their part to help clean up pollution. In this activity, your group can take a look at some pollution problems and then think of some ways they can help solve them. Start the activity by asking the kids to tell you what they think pollution is and where it comes from. Then use the background information in chapters two, three, and four to talk about some sources of pollution and the effects pollution has on people, wildlife, and the environment.

Next pass out a copy of page 79 and discuss the pollution problems on the page using the information in "Problems and Solutions" below. Ask the kids if they can think of any solutions to these problems. Then pass out copies of page 80. Explain that the pictures on the page show some solutions to the problems they just talked about. Have the group match each solution with the appropriate pollution problem and discuss how each solution helps solve the problem (see answers below).

After you discuss the solutions, give the kids time to color both pages. When they've finished, tell them to cut out one of the problem squares and fold it up along the dashed line at the top of the square to form a tab. Then they should put a few drops of glue on the back of the tab and carefully place the problem square over the appropriate solution square. (Make sure they put glue only on the tab.) Have them repeat this procedure for the rest of the problem squares. Then they can lift up the problem squares to see the pollution solutions underneath.

ANSWERS: 1—B, 2—A, 3—D, 4—C

ACTION TIP!

POLLUTION

PLEDGES

Have the kids make up their own pledges to help fight pollution. Pass out construction paper or drawing paper and tell the kids to write "I Pledge to" in the middle of their papers. Then have them fill in their own pollution-fighting ideas or use one of the suggestions from the activity. The kids can also illustrate their pledges. Afterward post all the pledges on a "Pollution Solutions" bulletin board.

PROBLEMS AND SOLUTIONS

Problems

1. Throwing away aluminum cans wastes energy and natural resources and adds to the solid waste problem.

2. When people drive cars and trucks, they create air pollution and traffic congestion. They also use energy (gasoline).

3. Throwing away a paper bag each day wastes energy and natural resources (trees) and contributes to the solid waste problem. Using disposable drink containers also contributes to the solid waste problem.

4. Most of the electricity people use in the U.S. comes from power plants that burn coal or oil. Burning these fossil fuels contributes to acid rain and other kinds of air pollution, and the extraction of these fuels can harm natural areas. The more electricity we use, the more pollution we create.

Solutions

A. By taking public transportation, carpooling, and riding bikes instead of driving their cars, people can help reduce air pollution and save energy.

B. Recycling aluminum cans saves energy and natural resources, and prevents more trash from being dumped in landfills.

C. By using only as much electricity as they really need, people can reduce the amount of air pollution produced by power plants. Using less electricity also helps to conserve fossil fuel supplies and preserve natural areas.

D. Carrying your lunch in a reusable lunch box or a cloth bag instead of a throwaway paper bag saves trees and the energy needed to produce more paper products; it also prevents more trash from being added to landfills. And using a Thermos instead of a throwaway drink container saves resources and reduces waste.

Clean Up Your Act!

Take action to reduce pollution.

Objective:
Describe several ways to help reduce pollution.

Ages:
Intermediate and Advanced

Materials:
- *chalkboard or easel paper*
- *see activity for suggestions*

Subjects:
Social Studies, Science, and Art

By starting an anti-pollution campaign in your classroom or meeting area, you can help your kids become aware of what they can do to fight pollution. After they've completed the 10-step countdown outlined below, they can continue their pollution-fighting efforts by participating in an action project to help clean up pollution in their community. We've listed some project ideas on page 74. (You can do steps 9-3 of the countdown in any order. But before you start the countdown, read through each step to see what materials you'll need.)

THE COUNTDOWN

10! CHART YOUR COURSE

Make a chart with the three headings "Problems, Causes, Solutions" and put it where everyone can see it. Explain to the kids that they'll be taking part in a pollution countdown to help reduce pollution and that they'll be using this chart to record the steps they take. Tell the kids that as they proceed with the countdown, they'll learn about a variety of pollution problems and ways to help solve them. Have the kids take turns updating the chart as they take on each of the following steps in the countdown.

9! ANTI-LITTER BUGS

Have the kids keep an eye out for litter, and tell them to be sure they clean up when paper, broken pencils, and other litter collect in the area. (Point out that, whenever possible, the kids should recycle or reuse the things they pick up.) The kids can create colorful "litter patrol" buttons to wear or signs to put on their desks. (Encourage them to use recycled materials for their buttons and signs.)

8! SUPPLY SPIES

Tell your group that people use many products every day that can cause pollution. For example, many cleaning products contain toxic ingredients, such as ammonia, that can contaminate water supplies when washed down the drain. Have the kids find out if any of the materials used in your classroom or meeting area contain toxic ingredients. (The April 1988 issue of *Ranger Rick* has a chart on pages 40-41 that lists many toxic supplies used in homes and schools, along with suggestions for alternatives. You can also order a "House-hold Hazardous Waste Wheel" from the Environmental Hazards Management Institute. See page 85 for more information on nontoxic alternatives.) The kids can also check with the maintenance staff to see which products are used and whether these products contain toxic chemicals. Then have the kids come up with a list of recommended alternatives to the toxic products currently used.

7! PLANT POWER

Explain to your group that *indoor* air pollution can be a big problem in some buildings. That's because pollutants from glues, new carpeting, toxic cleaning products, and other sources can become concentrated inside poorly ventilated buildings. (For more about indoor air pollution, see the box on page 35.)

Tell the kids that some kinds of houseplants absorb certain air pollutants and help to improve indoor air quality. Some of the best pollution absorbers are *Philodendrons*, gerbera daisies, golden pothos, and spider plants. You can ask a local garden center or nursery to donate plants or cuttings of these plants, and then have the kids take turns caring for them.

6! LIGHT THE WAY

Explain to the kids that every time they flick on a light switch or run hot water, they're using electricity. And this electricity use is probably contributing to pollution. That's because most electricity is supplied by coal- or oil-burning power plants, which emit harmful materials into the air. Point out to the kids that by using less electricity, they can help reduce pollution. Have the kids design eye-catching mini-posters that they can put near light switches to remind people to turn off lights when they're not needed.

5! MORE ENERGY ALERTS

There are probably lots of other ways to save energy in your meeting area. One thing you can look for is drafty windows. The kids can block drafts by caulking the area around the window. You can also contact your local utility company to see if they'll send a representative to talk to your group about ways to save energy.

4! THE LUNCH BUNCH

Talk with your kids about the amount of trash they generate at lunch and snack times. (To illustrate this point, you might want to collect all the garbage your group produces in one day.) If the kids bring their lunches, they can avoid throwing away a paper bag each day by packing their lunches in reusable lunch boxes or cloth bags. And instead of using disposable drink containers, they can bring drinks in a Thermos or other reusable container.

Another way to cut down on trash at meals and at parties is to keep a reusable plate handy. And if your cafeteria uses paper cups, plastic foam plates, or other throwaway materials, encourage officials to switch to reusable plates and utensils.

philodendron

spider plant

3! WASTE WATCHERS

To help cut down on the number of paper towels they throw away, the kids can bring in some rags from home. They can use these rags to clean up desks and tabletops, and then take turns washing them out in the sink or taking them home to be washed.

Other waste-watching tips include using both sides of a piece of paper before throwing it away or recycling it, setting up containers to collect pencil stubs that can be reused, and using construction-paper scraps for bookmarks and for art projects. And you can help watch waste by using both sides of the paper when copying handouts.

2! MEDIA MANIA

As your group nears the end of the countdown, have the kids publicize their achievements by writing articles for school and local newspapers, making posters, and organizing tours of their model meeting area. They may also want to write up an anti-pollution tip sheet for visitors to take home at the end of their tour.

1! CHECK THE CHART

As the last step in the pollution countdown, have the kids look over the Pollution Chart to decide whether they solved all the pollution problems listed. Discuss what worked and what didn't, and decide what projects the kids would like to continue. Was it possible to completely eliminate all forms of pollution? The kids will probably find out that it's nearly impossible to completely eliminate pollution—but that their pollution countdown did make a difference!

0! BLAST OFF!

When your group has reached the end of the pollution countdown, celebrate with an anti-pollution party! Put up decorations made from recycled materials. Avoid using balloons, since they can sometimes harm wildlife after being discarded. And be sure to serve party snacks on reusable dishes!

(continued next page)

BRANCHING OUT: TAKE ACTION IN YOUR COMMUNITY

Below we've listed some ideas for projects that you and your kids might want to take on to help solve pollution problems in your community. Before deciding on a project, you might want to show the kids "Special Report: You Can Make a Difference," a video that features kids around the country taking action to help protect the environment. An "Action Guide" that includes a detailed explanation of how to organize an action project accompanies the video. For more information, see "Films, Filmstrips, Slides, and Videos" on page 84.

Then, after the kids choose a project, take them on a fact-finding field trip to help them learn more about your community's pollution problems and potential solutions. Here's a list of places you might want to visit:

- landfill
- sewage treatment plant
- recycling center
- industrial plant
- incinerator
- power plant
- major development project or site of a proposed project
- nature center or wildlife rehabilitation center

PROJECT IDEAS

Fight Solid Waste
- sponsor a community litter pickup
- convince school officials and local businesses to buy products made from recycled materials
- educate your community about the benefits of recycling
- help set up a community composting program
- organize a boycott of throwaway products, such as disposable cameras and razors

Spare the Air
- sponsor tree-planting to help improve habitat and absorb carbon dioxide, a major greenhouse gas
- set up an acid rain monitoring program
- organize an alternative transportation day and encourage people to walk, bike, or use public transportation for that day

Clean Up the Water
- adopt a stream, river, lake, or beach, and clean it up
- monitor the water quality in a local river or stream (see page 65)
- educate your community about the effects of dumping waste down drains and into waterways

Work for Wildlife
- help others learn about laws that protect local species and their habitats
- work to set aside a local natural area as a park
- clean up a park, refuge, or other natural area

Tackle Toxics
- organize a community household toxic collection day
- design posters and fliers that educate the community about safer alternatives to pesticides
- publish an alternative products list for shoppers and distribute it at local stores

USDA—Soil Conservation Service

Challenge Technology!

Create ways to improve or replace current technologies, and then look at some real pollution-fighting inventions.

Objectives:
Define technology. Describe some advantages and disadvantages of current technologies. Identify some careers associated with pollution prevention and cleanup.

Ages:
Intermediate and Advanced

Materials:
* *copies of page 81*
* *copies of the challenges on page 76*
* *drawing paper*
* *crayons or markers*

Subjects:
Science, Social Studies, and Art

Here's an activity that will encourage your kids to think about the advantages and disadvantages of some of today's technologies. Begin by asking the kids to explain what the word "technology" means. Discuss their ideas, and then explain that technology is the application of science to solve problems. Have the kids come up with some examples of modern technologies. (cars, power plants, genetic engineering, computers, and so on) Point out that although technological advances have helped make life easier in many ways, they've also introduced new problems. For example, cars provide people with personal freedom, and they've made it possible to travel long distances in relatively short periods of time. But cars create problems too. Ask the kids if they can describe some problems associated with cars. (cause air pollution; result in human death and injury; require the building of roads, which destroys habitats; and so on)

Then explain that people are just discovering how some of the technologies we've created can harm the environment. For example, many scientists believe that acid rain, caused by pollutants released from coal-burning power plants and motor vehicles, is affecting the health of forests and lakes in some areas.

Tell the kids that some people are working to improve existing technologies and to develop new technologies that can help solve some of our environmental problems. Explain that the kids will be getting a chance to invent their own pollution-solving technologies. Give each person a copy of the "Technology Challenges" on page 76. Explain that the information describes some problems associated with different forms of technology that we use today. Then divide the group into six teams and assign each team one of the challenges.

Have the kids in each team read about their technology and then brainstorm some ideas to address their challenge. The ideas they come up with can include improvements on the current technology, or they can be entirely new types of technology. Emphasize that there are no right or wrong

answers to the challenges and encourage the kids to think as creatively as possible. Also have the kids illustrate their solutions and write down a few sentences that explain how they work.

When everyone has finished, have each team present its solutions to the rest of the group. Encourage the kids in the audience to ask questions and offer comments after each presentation. If the kids come up with a new kind of technology, discuss how it might introduce new pollution problems. Also have the kids consider other solutions to their challenge. For example, instead of making new types of cars that don't pollute as much, it might be better to design a city where people don't have to travel so far every day.

Next pass out a copy of page 81 to each person, and explain that the cartoon illustrations represent some real solutions to existing pollution problems. Use the information under "Pollution-Fighting Technologies" on page 76 to explain how each invention works and the disadvantages of each one. Then have the group discuss these questions:

* Do you think we can rely on new technologies to solve all our pollution problems? Why or why not? (Answers will vary. Point out that new technologies often introduce new pollution problems and, in some cases, act as "Band-aids" to temporarily deal with problems without addressing the real solutions.)

* Are there ways to solve pollution problems without developing new technologies? (Yes. People can change their behaviors. For example, people can cut down on the amount they drive by using public transportation or by riding their bikes more often.)

* Do you think we really need all the technologies we have? Why or why not? (answers will vary)

* What kinds of professions might be involved in finding solutions to pollution? (See the professions listed under "Branching Out" on page 77.)

(continued next page)

TECHNOLOGY CHALLENGES

1. Toxic Roads: During the winter, snow and ice can build up on roads, making it dangerous for people to drive. Snow-plowing removes only some of the snow and ice, so a special kind of salt is also spread on many of the roads to melt the rest. But when the snow and ice melt, the salty water runs off into lakes, rivers, streams, and other waterways. This salty runoff can kill fish and other animals, affect the growth of plants, and contaminate drinking water.
Your challenge: Invent a better way to make roads safe for travel during snowy winters.

2. Traffic Troubles: In many cities, cars are the major means of transportation. They're also one of the major causes of air pollution. With so many people driving their cars every day, there's a lot of traffic. A great deal of air pollution is created by the cars while they're stuck in traffic.
Your challenge: Invent a better form of transportation.

3. Pesty Poisons: Many farmers use pesticides to kill insects that damage their crops. Unfortunately, these pesticides often harm birds and other animals. Pesticides also contaminate water supplies.
Your challenge: Invent a safer way to control crop-eating insects.

4. Overdoing It: To keep fruit from being damaged during shipping, it's often placed on plastic foam trays and then wrapped in more plastic. But when the plastic is thrown away, it ends up in landfills that are already overflowing with garbage. And many toxic by-products are created when plastic is manufactured.
Your challenge: Invent a better way to package fruit to keep it from being damaged during shipping.

5. Don't Be Fuel-ish: Many power plants burn coal or oil to produce electricity. But burning these fuels results in air pollution. And getting these fuels out of the ground damages wildlife habitat. Natural areas can also be affected by accidents that occur when oil is being transported.
Your challenge: Come up with a less-polluting way to create energy.

6. Danger Indoors: In an effort to cut down on the energy needed to heat and cool buildings, many modern buildings have been designed to be as airtight as possible. But many pollutants can accumulate inside these "closed" buildings. (These pollutants are released by sources such as copy machines, cigarette smoke, new furniture, and cleaning chemicals.) In fact, the air pollution inside some buildings is much worse than it is outside! This indoor air pollution has made some workers sick.
Your challenge: Invent a way to reduce indoor air pollution without increasing the amount of energy used to heat and cool a building.

POLLUTION-FIGHTING TECHNOLOGIES

Super Bulbs: Energy-efficient, compact fluorescent bulbs use one-quarter of the energy of standard incandescent bulbs, and they last up to 10 times longer. By decreasing the demand for electricity, these bulbs can help reduce air pollution. But compact fluorescent bulbs are more expensive than incandescent bulbs, and they come only in lower wattages.
Goop Gobblers: Scientists have discovered strains of bacteria that feed on oil and other toxic pollutants. Bacteria have been used to clean up chemical spills and agricultural runoff. But sometimes the bacteria work too slowly—or not at all. And some scientists are concerned that introducing bacteria into areas where they aren't naturally found may disrupt local ecosystems.
Philodendron Filters: Scientists have discovered that common household plants such as *Philodendrons*, spider plants, and gerbera daisies can absorb some indoor air pollutants.

Bug-Vac: In California, some strawberry growers are experimenting with a safer alternative to pesticides. By attaching a giant vacuum, called a "Bug-Vac," to their tractors, they can suck bugs off their crops without damaging the fruit—and without using pesticides that can poison other animals and contaminate water supplies. But the Bug-Vac also removes some insects that don't harm crops.
Wave Catchers: A floating device called the "SEA Clam" captures wave energy in the sea. Waves press against SEA Clam's air bags, squeezing air through a valve and into a chamber where it spins a turbine that generates electricity. The SEA Clam equipment is expensive and can be used only in areas that have suitable waves.
Wacky Windmills: Modern windmills have been specially designed to efficiently catch the wind and use it to produce electricity. Wind-generated electricity doesn't create air pollution, but it's sometimes more expensive and less reliable than electricity

produced by burning fossil fuels. (New turbine designs and blade shapes may make them more efficient in the future.) Some people complain that windmills ruin scenic areas.
Sun-Mobiles: Instead of burning gasoline and polluting the air, solar-powered cars capture and use the energy from sunlight. Solar cells mounted on the cars turn this energy into electricity. On cloudy days, drivers keep their cars going by using extra energy from sunnier days that's stored in the car's battery. Currently, solar cars are expensive to manufacture and don't go as fast as gasoline-powered cars.
Smoke Scrubbers: In some coal-burning power plants, machines called *wet scrubbers* spray lime and water into smoke entering the smokestacks, rinsing out sulfur dioxide (a pollutant that causes acid rain) before it leaves the smokestack. This keeps most of the sulfur dioxide from getting into the air, but can leave a toxic sludge that must be disposed of.

Help your kids focus on the future by getting them to think about careers in pollution control and prevention. Copy the following professions on a chalkboard or sheet of easel paper: writer, newspaper reporter, teacher, engineer, farmer, automobile designer, politician, homemaker, sanitation engineer, lawyer, city planner, architect. Then, for each profession, have the kids brainstorm how a person could use his or her profession to help prevent or control pollution. For example, a teacher might specialize in teaching classes about the environment. You might also want to discuss what kind of training each profession requires, and add to the list any other professions the kids can think of.

After your discussion, arrange to have a "pollution professional" come in and talk to the kids. Contact local environmental organizations and state agencies for the names of individuals who might be willing to speak to your group.

Going Green

Create advertisements for products that are better for the environment than existing products.

Objectives:
Name some pollution problems associated with various products. Explain how consumers can cut down on environmental problems by being careful about what they buy.

Ages:
Intermediate and Advanced

Materials:
* *chalkboard or easel paper*
* *slips of paper*
* *research materials (optional)*

Subjects:
Social Studies and Art

ll kinds of products are "going green" these days. Companies are finding out that being sensitive to environmental concerns is a selling point, and many of them are changing their products and marketing to keep up with the trend.

By creating ads for "green products," your kids can learn about some of the ways companies are responding to the public's growing concern about pollution and other environmental problems. They'll also get a feeling for the ways their own consumer choices affect the environment.

Before you begin, write each type of product listed on page 78 on a separate slip of paper. Also copy the questions under "Product Particulars" on a chalkboard or sheet of easel paper where everyone can see them. Then start the activity by dividing the group into teams of four or five and having each team pick one of the slips. Give the teams time to brainstorm and, if necessary, research some ways their product might cause pollution. Tell them to think about all aspects of their product, using the questions under "Product Particulars" as general guidelines. Also have them think of other aspects of their product that might contribute to pollution.

Next tell the kids that each team will be responsible for coming up with an ad campaign that focuses on a "new, im-

proved" version of each product. To do this, the kids should think of ways that their products could be made less environmentally damaging. Then they should incorporate their ideas into an ad or series of ads that they'll present to the rest of the group. For example, the kids can draw colorful posters, write a jingle, or act out a TV or radio commercial.

After each team's presentation, discuss some of the pros and cons of the "improved" products. Also discuss whether these products will really be better for the environment or will simply cause other pollution problems. For example, the "milk group" might have advertised their new product as being better for the environment because the plastic jug it comes in is degradable. But many scientists are skeptical about how the word "degradable" is used. (See "Beware of Buzzwords" below for more information.)

After all the teams have made their presentations, tell the kids that some companies really are developing products that are less harmful to the environment. For example, one company sells concentrated fabric softener in small cardboard cartons. Consumers can buy the cartons, pour the concentrate into the empty plastic fabric softener jug, and add water. By purchasing the cardboard fabric softener refills instead of another plastic jug, consumers can cut down on plastic waste.

Also point out to the kids that, while some companies are making an effort to have less of an environmental impact, others are taking advantage of the "popularity" of environmental concern by making misleading or inaccurate statements about their products. (See "Beware of Buzzwords.")

To wrap up your discussion, ask the kids if they can think of ways individuals can avoid or cut down on the pollution problems associated with many consumer products. Use the information under "Be a Supermarket Activist" in the margin to reinforce their ideas.

As a follow-up, take the kids on a field trip to a grocery store to look for "green" products, as well as products that may have some pollution problems but that could be made less harmful to the environment. Also look for products that might have misleading (or even inaccurate) claims. For

example, certain products that are available in spray cans, such as some hair sprays, have phrases such as "environmentally safe" printed on the can. It's not clear exactly what this means, but it could be a reference to the fact that the product contains no ozone-damaging CFCs. (In 1978, the use of CFCs was banned in most spray products in the U.S.) But what kinds of chemicals are used in the product *instead* of CFCs, and what effects might these chemicals have? What about the disposal of the empty can? Is it environmentally safe in a landfill?

PRODUCTS

- apples
- paper towels
- sink cleanser
- plastic trash bags
- laundry detergent
- shampoo
- microwave meal
- soda
- milk
- spray deodorant

PRODUCT PARTICULARS

- What is it made of?
- Where do the ingredients come from?
- What processes are used to get or make the ingredients?
- How is it made?
- How is it packaged?
- Is it reusable?
- Is it disposable?
- Is it recyclable?
- Is it safe and/or healthy?

ACTION TIP!

BE A

SUPERMARKET

ACTIVIST

- Buy products in recycled and/or recyclable containers.
- Don't buy overpackaged products.
- Let store managers know your concerns about the pollution problems caused by products.
- Write to companies to let them know how you feel about their products.
- Prevent packaging waste by buying products in large quantities instead of in individually wrapped servings.
- Buy items that will last, instead of products such as disposable razors, cameras, and other throwaway items.
- Try to buy local produce and other products instead of those brought in from far away (to cut down on energy use and air pollution problems caused by transportation).

BEWARE OF BUZZWORDS

"Degradable" is a word that's cropping up more and more these days. Something that's degradable can be broken down into smaller components by natural processes.

Given enough time, natural processes will break down anything (although, depending on the substance and the circumstances, it may take hundreds or thousands of years for decomposition to occur). No standard legal definition of the word (that is, one that advertisers must adhere to) has been estab-

lished, so technically speaking, just about any product can be labeled as degradable—even if it takes years for the product to decompose.

Besides degradable, other advertising "buzzwords" to watch out for include *nontoxic, natural, organic,* and *environment-friendly.* Again, there are no legal guidelines for how these words can be used, so advertisers can—and sometimes do—use them very liberally.

1

2

3

4

A

B

CANS

C

D

Challenge Technology!

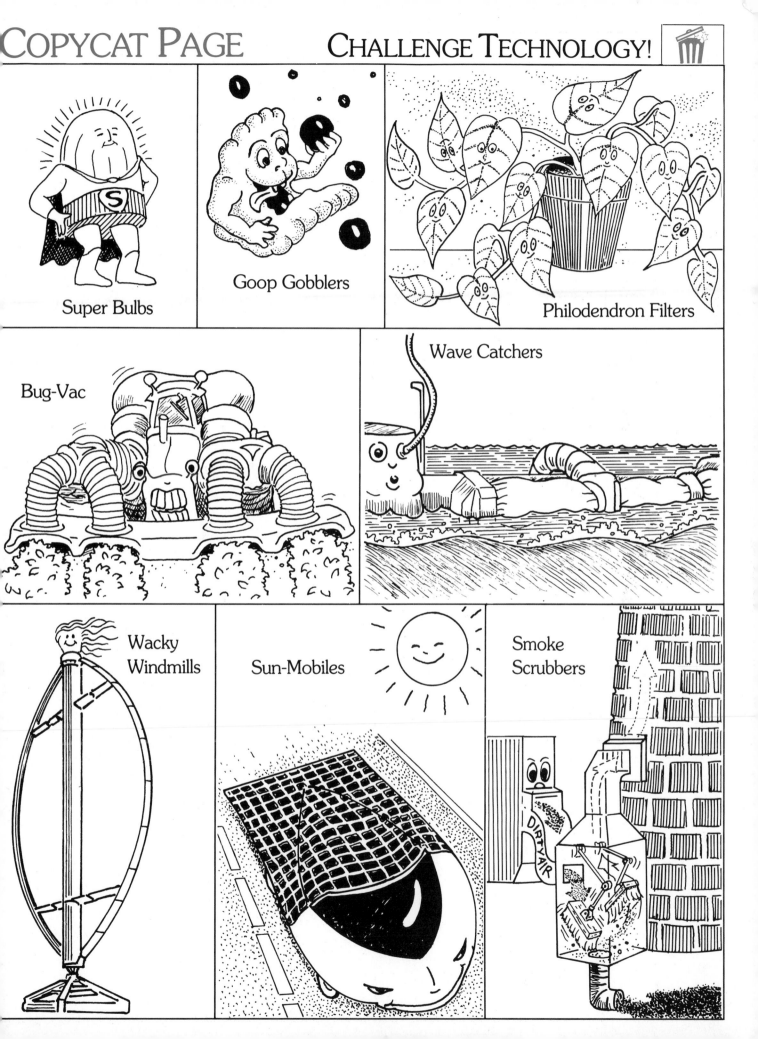

Super Bulbs

Goop Gobblers

Philodendron Filters

Bug-Vac

Wave Catchers

Wacky Windmills

Sun-Mobiles

Smoke Scrubbers

DIRTY AIR

Glossary

acid rain—precipitation that forms in the atmosphere when certain pollutants mix with water vapor. Acid rain, more accurately called *acid deposition,* can be in the form of rain, snow, sleet, hail, fog, or dry particles. The major sources of acid rain are sulfur dioxide and nitrogen oxide emissions from fossil fuel-burning power plants and motor vehicles.

biodegradable—having the ability to be broken down into simpler components by living organisms.

chlorofluorocarbons (CFCs)—chemicals that are used to produce plastic foam, coolants, and many other products. CFCs are the major cause of ozone depletion and are also one of the major greenhouse gases.

fossil fuels—coal, oil, and other energy sources that formed over millions of years from the remains of ancient plants and animals. Fossil fuel use is a major cause of pollution.

global climate change—the predicted change in the earth's climate brought about by the accumulation of pollutants in the atmosphere. The effects of global climate change could include altered weather patterns and rising sea levels.

greenhouse effect—the trapping of heat by gases, such as carbon dioxide, in the earth's atmosphere.

groundwater—water that fills the spaces between rocks and soil particles underground. Groundwater is replenished when rainwater trickles through the soil. *Surface water,* such as lakes and rivers, is often replenished by groundwater.

leaching—the process by which materials on or in soil are dissolved and carried by water seeping through the soil. Leaching may contaminate groundwater supplies.

ozone—a form of oxygen. *Low-level ozone,* the main ingredient in smog, is found near ground level and is produced when sunlight stimulates a reaction between pollutants. The *ozone layer* is a protective layer of ozone high in the earth's atmosphere that filters out much of the sun's harmful ultraviolet radiation. The *ozone hole* is the thinning of this layer caused by the release of chlorine atoms from chemicals such as CFCs.

PCBs (polychlorinated biphenyls)—chemicals that can build up to toxic levels in animal tissue.

point pollution—pollution that comes from a particular source, such as from a factory or sewage treatment plant. *Nonpoint pollution,* which doesn't come from a single, identifiable source, includes materials that wash off streets, lawns, farms, and other surfaces.

pollution—a human-caused change in the physical, chemical, or biological conditions of the environment that creates an undesirable effect on living things.

renewable resource—a resource that can be replaced through natural processes if it is not overused or contaminated. For example, water and trees are renewable resources. *Nonrenewable resources* are in limited supply and cannot be replenished by natural processes, at least not for thousands of years. Fossil fuels are a nonrenewable resource.

risk assessment—a process that analyzes the short- and long-term risks posed by certain technologies.

runoff—water, including rain and snowmelt, that runs off the surface of the land and into rivers, streams, and other water supplies. Runoff from farms, lawns, golf courses, and other development often carries traces of fertilizers, pesticides, and other toxic substances.

smog—low-level ozone, soot, sulfur compounds, and other pollutants in the atmosphere that cause poor visibility and create hazardous conditions for living things.

solid waste—discarded solid or semi-solid material, such as paper, metals, and yard waste. The *solid waste stream* is the sum of all the solid waste that is continuously thrown away.

sustainable development—development that uses resources in an efficient way and without destroying the basis of their productivity. For example, sustainable agricultural practices avoid the use of pesticides and chemical fertilizers that can pollute the soil and water.

toxic—a poisonous substance.

Pollution Laws And What They Do

Here's a summary of some of the most important pollution-control laws in the U.S. Many of these laws are enforced by the Environmental Protection Agency (EPA), a federal agency that was created in 1970.

Federal Insecticide, Fungicide, and Rodenticide Control Act (FIFRA): (1947, last amended 1988) Requires all pesticides to be registered with the EPA. The EPA can restrict or ban the use of any pesticide, and a pesticide already on the market can be suspended or banned if evidence of harmful effects turns up. FIFRA also states that a pesticide can remain on the market if its benefits outweigh its risks.

FIFRA has been used to restrict or ban pesticides such as DDT and heptachlor, but the law's effectiveness has been questioned because it takes so long to ban a pesticide. Also, many of the chemicals used in pesticides have not been tested to determine their effects on people and wildlife.

Federal Water Pollution Control Act: (1948, last amended 1987) Also known as the Clean Water Act. The act directs the EPA to establish discharge standards for factories, sewage plants, and other point sources of water pollution. States must issue permits to these point sources. The act also requires the EPA to monitor water quality on a national basis and to fund the construction and improvement of municipal wastewater treatment facilities. In 1987 amendments to the law were passed to address non-point pollution and toxic pollution, but it's not yet clear if these new laws are significantly reducing the effects of these types of pollution.

National Environmental Policy Act (NEPA): (1970) Requires federal agencies to prepare environmental impact statements for all proposed legislation or projects that could significantly affect the quality of the environment. As a result of these reports, plans for many dams, highways, and other development projects have been changed or cancelled. The act also established a three-member Council on Environmental Quality that determines the condition of the environment on an annual basis and that develops and recommends new policies to the president.

Clean Air Act: (1970, last amended 1977) Directed the EPA to set national air-quality standards for six major air pollutants: lead, particulate matter, sulfur oxides, carbon monoxide, nitrogen oxides, and chemicals that contribute to ozone formation. These standards specify the maximum allowable level of each pollutant in outdoor air, and are implemented through state plans. In addition, the act directs the EPA to set limits on the amount of pollution that can be produced by motor vehicles and newly constructed or expanded plants and to set national emission standards for toxic air pollutants. (By 1986, standards for only eight of the hundreds of potentially toxic pollutants had been set.)

Amendments proposed in 1990 call for greater control of toxic pollutants, for tighter air-pollution standards for cars, and for reductions in sulfur dioxide and nitrogen oxides to help prevent acid rain.

Ocean Dumping Act: (1972, last amended 1988) Set up a permit system to regulate ocean dumping.

A 1988 amendment requires phasing out the dumping of sewage sludge, industrial waste, and infectious medical waste into ocean waters.

Safe Drinking Water Act: (1974, last amended 1986) Requires the EPA to set maximum levels for all contaminants in drinking water that can affect human health. Public water supplies must be monitored to check for these contaminants. (Private wells are not regulated under the act.) Amendments passed in 1986 require the EPA to set standards for more than 80 pollutants in an attempt to speed up the EPA's slow progress in establishing drinking-water standards. So far, only a few of these new standards have been set and enforcement of the act remains poor.

Resource Conservation and Recovery Act (RCRA): (1976, last amended 1984) Stated that all open dumps in the U.S. had to be closed or upgraded to landfills by 1983. RCRA calls for the EPA to identify which chemicals qualify as hazardous waste, and to issue standards and permits for hazardous waste treatment, storage, and disposal. RCRA also provides funds to help states set up their own solid waste management programs. Amendments passed in 1984 call for phasing out hazardous waste disposal on land, but the effectiveness of these amendments has been questioned.

In addition, RCRA's effectiveness has been weakened because only a few of the many different kinds of hazardous waste are currently regulated. This means that many extremely toxic chemicals are still being dumped into the environment.

Toxic Substances Control Act: (1976) Controls the manufacture, use, and disposal of toxic substances. It calls for the EPA to create an inventory of all major chemicals made by or used in U.S. industries, to screen all new chemicals, and to ban those that pose an unreasonable risk to the environment.

Comprehensive Environmental Response, Compensation, and Liability Act: (1980, last amended 1986) Also known as Superfund. This act authorizes the EPA to require the cleanup of hazardous waste dumps. A multibillion-dollar fund, financed by the federal and state governments and by taxes on the chemical industry, provides money for the cleanups. Superfund authorizes governments to fine or sue those responsible for creating hazardous waste sites for cleanup costs and for damage to natural resources.

Although Superfund has focused public attention on hazardous waste disposal, it has been weakened by mismanagement and by budget cuts. Recent efforts to improve the program include a court ruling that forces polluters to pay for restoring environments damaged by hazardous waste dumping.

Community-Right-to-Know Act: (1986) Gave citizens access to information about hazardous chemicals in their communities. The act requires industries to identify what chemicals are stored in a community and to explain the health effects of these chemicals. Under the act, industries and communities must use this information to design and test chemical accident emergency plans.

1998 UPDATE

TABLE OF CONTENTS

Green Schools

Barnwell Elementary

by Pattie Aronson,
Environmental
Education Committee
Chairman
and Nancy Carter,
Curriculum Support
Teacher

Barnwell Elementary, located just outside Atlanta in Alpharetta, Georgia, became a member of the town's Green School program in 1991. Three years later, it was certified by the National Wildlife Federation as a Schoolyard Wildlife Habitat. Since that time, this public school of 973 students has hosted many local PTA presidents, environmental chairpersons, and principals as they visited Barnwell to research an excellent example of an outdoor classroom environment.

The school continually seeks to improve its environmental education program and enhance its grounds in an environmentally friendly way through the use of Outdoor Learning Centers. The Centers promote active "hands-on" learning, develop environmental awareness, and foster creative and critical thought. Additionally, they have returned wildlife to their habitat, used plants and trees as teaching tools, addressed the property's erosion problems, and improved the school's aesthetics.

Due to Georgia's recent increased attention on water pollution, awareness of and concern for the future of the water supply has become a catalyst for school and community action. As a responsible citizen, Barnwell has chosen to "clean up its own backyard" by addressing the problem of erosion on the school grounds. For example, one of the Outdoor Learning Centers, the Rock and Hummingbird Garden, was built on a slope that had been eroding for several years. It has alleviated the continual wash of mud onto a playground and flow of sediment into a storm drain.

In addition, this garden provides a variety of food, shelter, and water sources for hummingbirds and other birds throughout the year. A local technical school donated most of the native plants grown from seed in their horticultural department, and the remainder came from one of our business partners, family donations, and campus transplants. Barnwell's active environmental group, Earth Savers, an after-school "club for kids who care about the Earth" sponsored by the National Wildlife Federation, participated in raising funds for and creating the garden.

Barnwell also has an Adopt-a-Tree project that supports reforestation efforts by allowing families to donate trees and plants to be planted on the school grounds.

Erosion and sediment pollution in storm drains was reduced by lining this former dirt ditch with concrete and planting the slope with sod and gardens. Most of the sod here and all over campus was retrieved as leftover or unusable from landscape companies.

Pattie Aronson. Courtesy of Barnwell Elementary School PTA. Printed with permission

School yard waste goes into making compost to enrich student gardens.

Other outdoor learning classrooms offer a variety of additional lessons. The Colonial Homestead has kitchen and perennial gardens, an orchard, sundial, and water well, all historically accurate. A Butterfly Garden, which includes nectar and host plants, a butterfly box and bath, and a cherry tree salvaged from a nearby construction site, provides meaningful experiences for students who raise monarch butterflies from caterpillar through chrysalis and release them in the garden. The Arboretum contains 69 trees in 31 varieties, all labeled, giving students the opportunity to study and appreciate the trees, and has bluebird houses, a bog area, tracking box, rock and brush piles, work station, bird feeders, bat boxes, and more. A Courtyard Pavilion includes 12 class gardens and a future lily pond for aquatic environmental and natural science studies, as well as inspiration for creative expression in the arts and humanities.

Just beyond the Arboretum, a 750-foot Nature Trail winds through 1 1/2 acres of undisturbed mixed pine and native hardwoods. Equipped with benches and tables constructed from recycled plastic, the trail provides seating for groups to meet for instructional activities. Recycled lot signs identify various plants and flowers.

The Kids' Garden with its raised vegetable and flower beds reinforces the importance of plants to the life cycle and the environment. The garden includes a compost bin for yard waste, that has been named as a Compost

Barnwell's garden beds are lined with old railroad ties and logs and all garden signs were likewise salvaged from the school's local business partners, reusing old materials that would otherwise be thrown away. Window boxes for classroom trailers and replacement planks for picnic tables were made from old wood, and work stations in the Arboretum used wood spools from the local power company.

Demonstration Site by the City of Alpharetta. Students of all grades watch over their classroom plots, test soil, and prepare compost mixtures in proper ratios to ensure a healthy crop. Hands-on lessons that include feast and famine, drought, disease, and nutrition are easily integrated into the instructional program.

At Barnwell's Weather Station, the students use a range of instruments to provide data for use in the prediction of weather patterns. Throughout the school year, students make pH counts for acid rain measurement and chart rain and snowfall, temperature, wind speed and direction, barometric pressure, and sky conditions. These activities enhance the science processes of observation, collection, and recording, and reinforce the importance of historical data.

In addition to the Outdoor Learning Centers, Barnwell has focused on recycling over the past two years—plastic grocery bags, greeting cards, newspapers, six-pack rings, telephone books, and yellow pages. The school is also participating in a pilot program for recycling all paper and aluminum products. This schoolwide venture, sponsored by the county and a local waste management company, will measure the results for use in determining the success of a proposed state school recycling program.

As an Adopt-a-Road sponsor, four times a year Barnwell takes responsibility for cleaning up litter from a one-mile stretch of road fronting the school.

Barnwell's annual pansy and yard bag sale promotes environmental efforts and raises necessary funds to continue them. A highly visible bulletin board communicates pertinent information on environmental issues within the school, community, nation and globe.

The key to Barnwell's success in its environmental program has been the level of commitment and support it receives from the school, PTA, and community, especially from Principal Debbie Reeves and PTA President Laura Dobbs. This support has shown itself not only in an ability to provide exceptional Outdoor Learning Centers but also to focus attention on the importance of environmental issues in an educational and meaningful way. Through education we have raised the consciousness and level of respect for the environment around us. Embodiment of the notion that, "If everyone does a little, we can achieve a lot," has given our children hope for the future, both in terms of themselves and the world in which they live.

Pattie Aronson

They may not be pretty, but these recycling bins work! Barnwell now recycles all of its in-school paper and plastics, cutting its non-recyclable trash in half.

Pattie Aronson

Oil Spills

by Carol J. Boggis

I live in Portland, a small and lovely city on the coast of Maine. Portland Harbor is a narrow triangle of ocean whose upper end is full of ducks and herons. Farther down, there are fishing boats, wharves, and shops. Seals, lobsters, and fish swim at the harbor mouth. It was a wonderful place—until the day a ship spilled oil all over the harbor.

It was a sunny, calm morning in late September, 1996, and I was headed with a class on a field trip. We were scheduled to tour a big oil spill cleanup ship that is stationed in Portland to protect against spills from the many tanker ships that bring oil here. But when we arrived at the dock, the excited crew told us the tour was off—they had an oil spill to go to! An oil tanker, trying to squeeze through the narrow opening under the bridge, had turned just the wrong way. It hit the bridge hard and was leaking oil. The cleanup crew couldn't take us along, since they had a big job to do, but they told us where the ship was.

We drove around the harbor to where the giant ship had pulled into dock. What a mess we saw there. The black and red-brown hull of the ship, looming high above us, showed a huge gash near the waterline. Thick black oil was pouring out of it, and oil was also gushing up from a second hole we couldn't see underwater. Oil was spreading out over the water in all directions. Cleanup workers were trying to corral the oil floating on the water with long *booms* of floating plastic hose, but there was too much oil and lots escaped. The smell of oil was strong and dizzying—like gasoline, only heavier, sweeter, and thicker. The smell spread with the breeze over the entire city for a whole day as some of the oil evaporated. We all stood on the shore, just watching, some students crying, as the oil spread farther and farther. How could this happen to our beautiful harbor?

By the next day, more booms had been put in place, and many boats large and small were sucking up some oil from the water with skimmers. But the oil

Carol J. Boggis

Michael S. Hamilton

Left: *The damaged tanker reveals a huge hole where its oil drained out. Smaller boats help clean up the oil spill.*
Above: *Floating oil filled inlets at high tide, then drained away at low tide, leaving marsh grasses completely covered with black oil.*

had been carried up and down the harbor with the tide and had washed onto the shore all along the edge where it is much harder to remove, like a horrible bathtub ring. Cleanup crews fought to keep the oil at least contained inside the harbor. About 180,000 gallons of two types of fuel oil had spilled, heavy black oil and light oil that spread fast in a thin, rainbow sheen over the surface.

I thought of all the otters, birds, and other animals that were covered with oil when the *Exxon Valdez* ran aground in Alaska in 1989. Would this happen here? I drove to several places around the harbor to look and didn't see much wildlife.

Then I came to a quiet cemetery. On a grassy bank at the water's edge was a cormorant, a long-necked fishing bird. Cormorants are black, but this one looked different than normal and acted different. He let me get very close, only a few feet away, and seemed mostly interested in preening, trying to clean his feathers—which I saw were oily and clumped together. He blinked, and his normally clear, dark eyes shone eerily green with a thin layer of oil. Cormorants are very big and strong, and have sharp beaks, so it would have been dangerous for him and me to try to catch him; I might have only scared him back into the oily water. I called on experts to help, but when I went back, the bird was gone. I never found out whether he lived or died.

Oil is toxic, to people as well as to wildlife. Cleaning up oil and rescuing wildlife has to be done by experts with protective clothes and equipment, for everyone's safety. Special treatment is needed for the wildlife, too, to counteract the effects of the poisonous oil and the stress of capture.

On the third day, the wind came up, and so did the tide. It pushed the oil two feet above usual high tide, coating the shore in places it hadn't reached before. Wind, waves, and currents pushed oil over and under the booms. Oil washed as far up the harbor as it could go, even into the Audubon bird sanctuary. I stood on a narrow bridge there and watched helplessly as the first ominous streamers of black oil trailed upstream into the sanctuary, wondering why no one could stop it.

Down the harbor, all along the inlets, the shoreline was covered with thick, black, stinking goo. The marsh grasses, usually green and gold, were coated a glistening, solid, midnight black. Where the oil mixed with sand, it slowly turned hard, in a process called asphalting (like on city streets).

Among the docks, the pilings were coated. The lobstermen had to throw away thousands of lobsters they had caught and kept in floating cages. Fishermen had to stop fishing around the harbor. No one could sail a boat through the oil, since this would spread it farther away. Boats at the docks had to be carefully washed off and the oil captured before it ran back into the water.

Some seals were seen poking their heads up through the floating oil, but none could be caught. Hundreds of gulls, ducks, and other water birds were seen with some oil on them, but most could still fly away and couldn't be caught, and many more oiled birds were just never seen. A few were brought in to a rehabilitation center, but over half of them died.

Carol J. Boggis

A cormorant with its feathers covered in oil.

Within a few days, the oil had mostly washed up onto shore. Though a large percentage had been sucked up off the water, lots was left. Next came the shoreline cleanup, which is hard and slow, and took hundreds of workers many weeks to do. Big hoses were used to spray oil off the rocks, and booms used to catch that oil. Workers hand–rubbed oil off rocks with absorbent towels, which along with disposable booms were burned in an incinerator to generate electricity. The oil that was sucked up was filtered and used for low-grade heating fuel in furnaces.

But some of the oil just couldn't be recovered. It's hard to face, but sometimes leaving it there may be the best choice, especially for fragile areas like marshes. Cleaning up shallows means walking on the mud, but that drives the oil deeper where it can't be broken down. Leaving it means that winter storms weather away some oil by ice and water, and much is broken down by microbes. Oil spills aren't permanent; it may take years, but their effects do disappear, though the long-term effects on the food chain are less well understood.

Now, a year later, how does the harbor look? From a distance, in the marsh upstream, not bad. The black goo is gone. Grasses grew back in most places, though there are thin patches and bare areas. But there's still some oil in the mud, and scientists are keeping track of how fast it's breaking down.

Along the wharves, fishermen, lobstermen, and others are back to work, and were paid for their losses by the ship's owners. The oily ring left on pilings and rocks is hardened and stable. People are starting to forget how bad it was . . .

And that's dangerous. It seems we only worry about something if it's a recent disaster. When the *Exxon Valdez* wrecked, it made many people all over the country realize that something like it could happen in their own harbors or along their own shores, anywhere that oil tankers went. They made plans to prevent oil spills and improved their readiness to clean them up. Their preparation made Portland's cleanup as successful as it was. The problem is never forgetting to *stay* ready.

Prevention and cleanup preparedness are both important. Preventing spills involves safer navigation, screening ships' safety records, and so on. Preparation for spills includes training cleanup workers; improving technology; mapping marshes, endangered species habitats, and other sensitive areas to protect; planning for rescuing wildlife; and many other things. It's important to keep improving our abilities, so that we can do better next time.

And there will be a next time, because people make mistakes. Every year, on average, there's an oil spill about this size somewhere in the U.S., and nine around the world, according to the *Oil Spill Intelligence Report*. We don't often hear about them, unless they happen to us. But we can learn from them.

Cleanup workers use hoses, booms, and pads to remove oil from the shore.

Carol J. Boggis

Oil Spill Cleanup

Create an oil spill in miniature and try to clean it off shorelines, water, and bird feathers.

Objectives:
Watch the interaction of oil, water, and floating objects. Test different methods of cleanup on land and water. Observe the effect of oil on bird feathers.

Ages:
Intermediate

Materials:
- *glass bottle or jar with cap*
- *water tinted with blue food coloring*
- *cooking oil colored with black tempera paint*
- *cork or toy boat that fits inside the bottle*
- *large pan*
- *sand*
- *cleanup materials: cotton balls or swabs, cut-up panty hose, paper towels, popcorn, sponges, sawdust, gauze pads, rope or string, turkey baster or eye dropper, popsicle sticks*
- *bird feathers*
- *clean water in small pan*
- *liquid detergent*
- *toothbrush*
- *hair dryer*

Subject:
Science

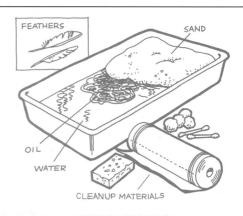

When oil spilled in Portland Harbor, schoolchildren had an environmental lesson they didn't expect. Some were very upset, and many had lots of questions. Their teachers found ways to turn the spill into useful lessons that helped them understand and learn about this major event. For instance, third-graders at Hall Elementary, who had been studying the upper marsh and testing its water quality monthly, visited the marsh soon after the spill. They assessed how much oil was present and saw less than they feared. They also did hands-on classroom activities like those below to see what oil spills were like. Like many other classes all along the Maine coast, they discussed wildlife, cleanup technology, and our reliance on oil. Some classes planned to study how well the marsh had recovered a year later.

Here are some activities to teach about oil spills. Who knows? By the time one happens where you live, what you began to learn here may help you save your own shore . . .

To demonstrate what happens in an oil spill, fill a glass bottle two-thirds full of water with food coloring. Pour 1/2 inch or more of black-tinted cooking oil into the bottle to represent the "oil spill." Where does the oil

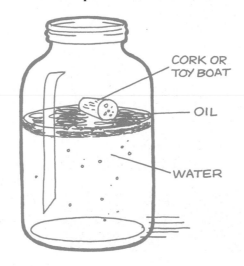

congregate (on the surface)? Drop the cork or toy boat in the bottle. What happens to it? (It becomes coated with oil.) Put on the cap and shake the bottle vigorously to simulate a storm or wave action. What happens to the oil? (Some mixes with the water.) Ask what would happen to organisms that float on the surface, such as sea birds, ducks, seaweed, or plankton, or that need to come to the surface to breathe, such as whales, seals, or sea turtles. (They'd be coated with oil.) Explain that over time water and oil mix somewhat and that some of the oil will sink to the bottom of the ocean. (Actual oil is heavier than this cooking oil.) What would happen to lobsters, crabs, sea urchins, and bottom-dwelling fish?

Next, students will try to clean up an oil spill before it pollutes the ocean, animals, and shoreline. In one end of the large pan, add a mound of sand to represent a sandy shoreline. Add blue-tinted water in the rest of the pan. Add black cooking oil to the water to simulate a spill. Let each team of three to four students choose two or three different cleanup materials to test. Have students make a plan for how they will use each material, then test them. Discuss why their efforts worked or didn't work. Was all the oil removed? How well might their methods work on an actual spill? What conditions would be different? Discuss what kinds of equipment actual oil spill cleanup personnel use, such as containment booms, skimmers, absorbent materials, etc. and how similar they are to items the students used.

Have the students make a diagram or list of the life in a marine environment near them. How would each organism be affected by an oil spill? What animals are most vulnerable to an oil spill (those that can't move; filter feeders like oysters, barnacles, and clams; those that surface often; those that depend exclusively on marine life for their food supply, etc)?

Next, examine what oil does to bird feathers. Examine a feather. Natural oiliness on the feather keeps it from becoming waterlogged.

Notice how it can fluff up after it's handled. Drop the feather into a pan of clean water. Does it float? Shake it off and dry it completely with the hairdryer. Does it still fluff up after being wet?

Now drop the feather into the pan of blue water and black oil. What happens to it? Use more than one feather and have student groups try to clean them up. Some students may use liquid detergent; others may just scrub with a toothbrush. Dry the feathers with the hair dryer. Do they still fluff up? Drop them into a pan of clean water. Do they still float as well as before? These tests indicate that the feathers have lost their ability to insulate and to resist water.

(Adapted with permission from "Save the Bay" on the Gulf of Maine Aquarium web page)

WHAT ELSE CAN YOU DO?

1. LEARN! about your local environment and industries. Ask questions. Investigate! Is oil brought here? How much? Who's in charge of safety and cleanup? How prepared are they for a spill? What wildlife lives in the area? Is it threatened by oil spills? Where and how should it be protected? Do the people in charge know where to protect wildlife? How do they plan to do it? Are they ready to rescue and rehabilitate wildlife? How?

2. TALK! to others. Use your knowledge to inform and persuade others to do all they can to prevent and cleanup spills. Spread the word with other kids. Talk to parents, teachers, and other adults; they can vote and have influence.

3. WRITE! letters to legislators and newspaper editors about what you've learned. Write to officials in charge of preparedness and ask them to improve in areas you're unhappy with.

4. FOLLOW UP! What can everyone do to reduce the risk of oil spills? Use less oil! That means fewer ships have to bring oil to harbor. It only takes the U.S. twenty seconds to use 200,000 gallons, the same amount as was spilled in Portland Harbor in the story. Energy conservation that saves oil can mean driving less and other ideas. See the articles in this issue called "Car Talk" and "Choices and Challenges" for more things we all can do to save energy.

GREEN + GLOBE = A Better World

One of the biggest changes in education over the last decade has been the increased use of computers and the Internet. Two organizations, GLOBE and GREEN, have combined scientific investigation of the environment with information-sharing via the Net to offer students a wider picture of their physical world.

The GLOBE Program focuses on the importance of gathering baseline information, which is vital to all scientific study, in areas relating to climate change, ozone depletion, acid rain, and others. Making sense of vast worldwide systems such as climate requires large-scale area studies, computers to compile enormous volumes of data, and sharing information worldwide. GLOBE introduces students to these concepts and tools.

The GREEN organization similarly uses scientific inquiry, but closer to home, to investigate pollution and other environmental problems in local communities. They use inquiry-based watershed education to involve students in scientific research with direct relevance to their lives. GREEN encourages students to take action on environmental issues in their communities, and provides tools to do so. These include software, videos, books, field manuals, kits for water tests and experiments, workshops, newsletters, and other guidance on the subjects of water and air pollution and monitoring.

GLOBE: GLOBAL LEARNING AND OBSERVATION TO BENEFIT THE ENVIRONMENT

by Ann Hardison

The lunch bell rings and a group of 12-year-olds in Spokane, Washington race to a small wooden shelter just outside their school building. They peer closely at a special thermometer hanging in the white shelter, carefully recording the high and low air temperatures for the past 24 hours. They then gaze upward, examining the sky to determine cloud type and density.

Across the country in Waldorf, Maryland, a group of middle schoolers bend down at the edge of a shaded pond to draw a water sample, precisely testing the water's temperature and acidity. Their classmates are digging in the soil nearby, taking samples to determine the soil type and moisture.

Using the Internet, the students in Washington and Maryland send their findings to a central collection center in Boulder, Colorado. Their data is combined with student data from schools around the world to create a global picture of our atmosphere, hydrosphere, and biosphere. With minutes, the students' work is posted on the World Wide Web at http://globe.fsl.noaa.gov.

This is not busywork. These are student-scientists gathering technically sound measurements that they, and

scientists, are using to learn more about the workings of our planet. They are part of a network of over 4,000 schools called GLOBE—Global Learning and Observation to Benefit the Environment.

"GLOBE joins the minds and hands of thousands of young people, teachers, and scientists around the world," said its founder, U.S. Vice President Al Gore. The Vice President initiated the GLOBE Program in April 1994 to help students reach higher levels of achievement in math and science while also increasing our understanding of Earth.

"The various GLOBE measurements, made over time, will allow the student to see on a local scale how the Earth's systems are interconnected in a dynamic and predictable way, producing an increased knowledge and understanding of how our planet works," explained Dr. Barry Rock, an associate professor at the University of New Hampshire.

Under the guidance of trained teachers, GLOBE students have already reported over 750,000 environmental observations. The students make measurements in atmosphere, hydrology, biology, and soils. Specific measurements include water turbidity, the temperature and pH of rain, and soil moisture. The students use Global Positioning System (GPS) devices to plot and report their exact location on the earth. This helps scientists using the data in their research.

"The GLOBE data are helping us define what an area is like now and the hope is that, over time, we will be able to see variations in the data that will tell us something about the climate of the region and whether or not we are seeing any evidence of change," explained Dr. Susan Postawko of the University of Oklahoma.

Teachers have given GLOBE high marks for motivating students. "GLOBE helps students with skills such as thinking critically, communicating effectively, demonstrating global responsibility, developing cross-cultural understanding, and accessing and using information effectively," reports Diane Duncan, a teacher in St. Charles, Illinois.

Learning doesn't stop with taking, reporting and studying various environmental observations on the Web. Through their own special E-mail system, GLOBE schools around the world contact each other to discuss education and science issues, such as how the current El Niño is being experienced at different locations. The students learn about each others' languages and cultures.

Recently, students in Australia challenged other GLOBE students to work with their local newspapers, encouraging them to publish tips on subjects such as recycling and responsible stewardship of natural resources. In the Czech Republic, a GLOBE school began recycling old paper and other rubbish to raise money for the purchase of a computer so they could send in their data reports via the Internet.

In Kingsburg, California, a group of GLOBE students and their teacher successfully petitioned the local land management agencies to reject a plan to develop one of the last remaining parcels of undisturbed land—which also happened to be their GLOBE study site. The authorities decided instead to move the area into permanent protected status.

GLOBE is beginning to build a presence in South American countries such as Ecuador. Andrea de Suarez of GLOBE Ecuador reports that they hope to expand the program into the Amazonian Rainforest and the Galapagos Islands. "The remarkable cultural and biological diversity of my country will allow us to collect data in a great variety of ecosystems and environmental conditions."

In the U.S., GLOBE is administered by a federal government interagency team that includes the National Oceanic and Atmospheric Administration, the National Aeronautics and Space Administration, the National Science Foundation, the Environmental Protection Agency, and the Departments of Education and State, working together with over 45 state and local partner organizations.

All U.S. K-12 schools are invited to join GLOBE. Participation requires a trained adult leader, Internet access, a computer, and specific measuring equipment. Broad international participation is integral to the design of the GLOBE Program. GLOBE international partners sign bilateral agreements with the U.S. for schools in their country to participate in the program.

For more information, contact the GLOBE Help Desk at 1-800-858-9947 or send E-mail to info@globe.gov.

GREEN: GLOBAL RIVERS ENVIRONMENTAL EDUCATION NETWORK

by Timothy Donahue

In the spring of 1984, students at Huron High School in Ann Arbor, Michigan, spoke with their teacher about some recent cases of hepatitis in their school. They noted that their sick friends enjoyed windsurfing on the Huron River in a nearby city park and wondered if the river was connected to the outbreak of disease.

The teacher and students brought their concerns to the attention of Professor William Stapp at the University of Michigan. Dr. Stapp brought graduate students, educators, and scientists together with the Huron High group. They got busy, following an original, interdisciplinary watershed education model known as GREEN.

By measuring changes in water quality over time, the Huron High students were able to document increases in fecal coliform levels in the river following storm events. (Fecal coliform bacteria indicate that raw sewage is entering a body of water.) The students alerted city and county health authorities, and were instrumental in creating a number of significant changes: The city immediately closed the windsurfer rental concession that had been operating in the park, and a

hinged sign was installed that could be opened following storms to reveal a message warning against bodily contact with the water. Later, a number of sewer lines from homes and businesses in the city were found to still be connected to the storm drainage system, in violation of more recent standards, and were promptly corrected. Residents of Ann Arbor eventually voted in favor of a tax increase to update and increase the capacity of the municipal sewage treatment facilities.

GREEN's watershed education model quickly spread to other schools along the Huron River, into other watersheds in the Great Lakes region of the United States and Canada, and across North America. In 1989, GREEN facilitated training workshops for educators and environmental groups in 18 countries in Africa, Asia, Europe, and Latin America, laying the groundwork for a truly global network.

Participants in GREEN collect and analyze local environmental data, while studying current and historical patterns of land and water usage within their watershed. They share data, concerns, and strategies for action with schools, community groups, scientists, resource managers, regulatory agencies, and government authorities within their watershed and beyond.

GREEN's education model synthesizes the content and process of learning by using inquiry-based investigation into the local environment as the vehicle for increasing student interest, motivation, and interdisciplinary content understanding. GREEN participants don't just talk about what to do with the results of their investigations—like the students at Huron High they develop critical problem-solving skills to formulate an appropriate plan of action and carry it out, thus making a real difference in their community.

The watershed is an excellent context for young and old to get to know the local environment. It teaches us how to integrate and analyze information from a variety of sources and perspectives and to take action based on what we have learned. Our network includes individuals and groups in more than 140 countries around the world.

For further information, contact:
GREEN
206 South Fifth Avenue, Suite 150
Ann Arbor, MI 48104 USA
Tel: 313-761-8142
Fax: 313-761-4951
Email: green@green.org
http://www.econet.apc.org/green/
For our online brochure, send a blank
   e-mail message to
   <green-info@igc.apc.org>

We All Live in Watersheds

by Carol J. Boggis

I n recent years, people have become more aware of the problem posed by nonpoint source pollution, including runoff from streets, farms, and other human activities. The chapter on "Troubled Waters" explains what happens when this runoff, and all the pollutants it carries, ends up in rivers, lakes, and the sea.

In the following activity, begin by handing out copies of the copycat page "Big Stream and Blue Lake" to the class. Then read the story below. At the end of Part One, tell the class you'll stop there, partway through the story, and ask them some questions. What was happening to Big Stream and Blue Lake in the story? What was causing the water to turn green and muddy? Was it any one problem, or many? Then explain that what happened in this story is the result of "nonpoint pollution." Use information from "Troubled Waters" to explain the term.

Tell them what happened to Big Stream and Blue Lake is happening every day, around the country. Though not everyone lives on the shore of a lake or stream, everyone lives in a watershed that drains somewhere, to a stream, river, lake, or ocean. So what we all do, on every inch of land, affects the waters we enjoy.

What can we do to prevent streams and lakes from turning Big Muddy and Green? Give each student a copy of "Shoreline Do's and Don't's", and introduce them as some ideas, especially for those who live near water, to reduce the pollution we create. Explain that many of these are things kids can do or teach others how to do. Go through the list and discuss the items. At the end, ask the class if they can think of other things they could do to help.

When you finish discussing the list, finish reading the rest of the story.

BIG STREAM AND BLUE LAKE: PART ONE

Big Stream fed into Blue Lake amid rolling hills, farms, and forests. The lake and stream were clear and cool, and huge trout lived in their depths. Their shores and waters were quiet and inviting on hot summer days, and people came from miles around to camp, swim, and boat on the lake, and canoe and fish on the stream. The water in the lake and swimming holes of the stream was so clean and pretty, people could take baths in it.

People liked the lake and stream so well, they wanted to stay longer and longer. Soon they began building cottages all along the shore, so they could stay all summer in comfort. New dirt roads went all around the lake, and driveways to the camps, and boat ramps to the water. When the best, most open flat shoreland was taken, the only places left had cliffs that came almost down to the water. But people built camps there anyway, sometimes using bulldozers to carve back the cliff a little more to make room, sometimes building right out over dirt they dumped in the lake to widen their spot.

WHAT DOES INQUIRY-BASED WATERSHED EDUCATION LOOK LIKE?

Doug and Janet's fourth and fifth grade classes travel to the Tonda Stream. Working in small groups, the children are pursuing investigations they have designed for themselves, based on their initial observations of the stream and its surroundings. One group stands at the water's edge, using a net to collect macroinvertebrates; a second group gathers in an adjacent field to draw an area map; and a third group surveys the surroundings to examine the conditions under which cocklebur plants thrive.

This vignette provides a snapshot of inquiry in process, not a complete picture of an inquiry-based classroom. To learn how the students and their teachers developed these investigations and how the students proceeded from here, examine some of Doug and Janet's reasons for choosing Tonda Stream as a site and some of their strategies for helping students devise questions and, eventually, design and conduct environmental investigations.

Doug and Janet knew that the many features of Tonda Stream and its surroundings could spark student interest. In fact, the range of possible investigations was one of the primary reasons they chose the site. Even though they recognized the potential for multiple investigations, Doug and Janet stopped short of deciding which aspects would be studied. Instead, they began teaching their students six phases of inquiry that could be used as a framework for designing and conducting investigations. Doug and Janet were careful to help students understand that the phases of inquiry were best used as guidelines, not as a rigid procedure to be followed sequentially.

After this introduction the students were asked to define these phases of inquiry in their own words. They developed the following definitions:

- Observing is "look[ing] at something keenly; and "pay[ing] close attention with your eyes."
- Questioning is deciding "what you would like to know."
- Formulating inquiry is "deciding what you want to do... designing[ing] a problem."
- Predicting is "taking what you know and guessing what's going to happen."
- Testing predictions includes "finding out if you are right," "testing your ideas," and "researching [and] collecting data."
- Concluding is "finding the answer if possible and then find[ing] new questions."

Once students demonstrated an understanding of the process of inquiry, they traveled to the study location to observe the stream and its surroundings and to generate their own questions about the site. These questions led to the formation of collaborative work groups, composed of students with similar interests. Within these groups, students refined their initial questions to develop specific, testable hypotheses and carry out investigations to test them.

(Adapted from Inquiry in Environmental Education: A Handbook for Elementary Teacher Enhancement, ©1997 by TERC and Global Rivers Environmental Education Network (GREEN)

They grew lawns and cut down trees to get a better view. They built docks out into the water, so they could use bigger motorboats. They piled sand to make beaches. Nobody worried much about all the outhouses along shore; the lake seemed so big it could hold everyone, and each one added seemed so small. But they got closer together, and noisier.

Weeds were cut down in some parts of the lake, so boat propellers wouldn't get tangled; people didn't seem to see ducks as much after that. But they still liked to come to the lake, and stayed there longer and longer. Pretty soon, they fixed up their cottages so they could stay year-round, adding showers, septic systems, and clothes washers.

Gradually, it seemed like the water wasn't so clear any more. Where once there had been pretty rocks visible on the bottom, now they were covered with brown slimy algae. In many places you couldn't see the bottom at all, and the water was a cloudy green. When boats roared by, kicking up big waves, the water close to shore got muddy from silt, and people came out from swimming feeling dirty. So they stopped swimming and bathing in the lake and took showers instead.

There were less fish, too, especially trout, who needed clear water to see the insects they ate. There were only more carp, who liked cloudy water and fed on the muddy bottom. So people gave up fishing. When it rained, the stream ran brown and carried more silt to the lake. Boats got stuck in the muck that built up, so people stopped boating.

People who had been coming to the lake for years began to feel that somehow it wasn't so special or fun any more. They wondered if they might have to change the name of Big Stream to Big Muddy, and Blue Lake to Green Lake. Wasn't there anything they could do?

PART TWO

People who loved Blue Lake and Big Stream realized what was happening. They found out that their pollution problems were caused, not by one big source, but by everyone. They began to learn what to do, and to take action.

They let their lawns go wild again, and stopped fertilizing them. That was easy! They planted beautiful trees and shrubs on the shoreline. They tested water all over, found where septic systems were leaking, and fixed them. They were careful what they washed down their drains. They stopped building new cottages so close to shore, and lined ditches with rocks and other materials. No new docks were built into the water, and they replaced docks with removable floats. They let weeds grow back in the shallows. They even found it easier to take care of their land this way. They learned boater courtesy and found it made everyone get along better. Farmers changed to ways of farming that limited runoff of fertilizer and soil.

Gradually, the shoreline began to look natural again. Cottages disappeared behind trees and shrubs as they grew taller. After storms, the stream ran a little muddy only for a little while, then soon clear again. Best of all, Blue Lake turned blue and clear again, trout came back, and ducks filled the marshy areas. People still came and enjoyed their lake, but had learned to take care of it, too.

- **BARE GROUND**—It's the top problem for many lakes. When soil erodes and runs off into a lake or stream, it carries phosphorus with it. Phosphorus is a natural element found in soil and rocks, and it works like fertilizer, causing algae blooms. Avoid disturbing soil any more than necessary, and don't leave ground scraped bare. On shoreline property, don't rake up leaves or pine needles; they help slow and absorb runoff.

- **LAWNS**—Reduce their area, or avoid planting them in the first place. Fertilize as little as necessary.

- **SHORELINE BUFFERS**—Keep, or plant, a strip of trees, shrubs, and other plants along shore. This acts to filter runoff before it reaches the lake. Not cutting down shoreline plants screens off cottages from the lake, making a nicer, more natural view for everyone.

- **PATHS**—Follow winding trails to the lake, not straight down, which hurries runoff into the water.

- **BEACHES**—Don't build beaches by dumping sand, as that adds tons of soil pollution directly to the lake, including phosphorus, and buries bottom habitat. Such beaches soon wash away, too. Enjoy the shoreline as natural as you found it.

- **AQUATIC WEEDS**—These rooted plants act as good fish habitat, trap sediments, and absorb phosphorus. Keep them around.

- **HUMAN WASTE**—Keep septic systems pumped and maintained, and follow regulations for waste disposal systems. When camping or boating, use latrines, not lakes or streams or anywhere within 100 feet of them.

- **CARS**—If you wash them near water, use only water, not detergents.

- **DOCKS**—Build only removable floats, not permanent docks. Use cedar, not pressure-treated or creosoted wood, as they leach poisons into the water.

- **BOATS AND JET SKIS**—Go slow near shore so as not to kick up waves. Stay out of shallows, unless you're in a canoe or rowboat. Be careful not to spill oil or gas, or drop litter, fishing line or sinkers. Maintain motors so they don't leak and cause air or water pollution; use fuel-efficient motors and pollution controls. Boats cause noise pollution, too, that disturbs wildlife and people; courtesy and good mufflers can help!

- **ROADS, DRIVEWAYS AND DITCHES**—Add ditches along dirt driveways to limit erosion, then line them with stone or grass. Channel ditches into flat woods, fields, or basins to give the water a place to soak into the ground slowly. Check for problem areas during a rainstorm by looking for brown runoff.

- **NEW CONSTRUCTION**—Never build closer than 100 feet to shore, or on steep slopes. Don't fill in the lake to build out over the water. Disturb only the smallest area necessary at one time. Use hay bales or silt fences to trap sediment downslope. Minimize cleared or paved areas. Runoff from residential and commercial land allows 5 to 30 times the phosphorus runoff into waterways as undisturbed forests.

- **FARMS**—Agriculture can be a big contributor to rural lake pollution. Fertilizers increase plant production *everywhere* they are, including algae in a lake. Use only as much as needed. Store fertilizer and manure carefully to prevent runoff. Avoid pesticide use wherever possible. Prevent soil erosion, and keep livestock away from waterways. These ideas apply to lakeside gardeners, too.

- **TEACH OTHERS**—Talk to your neighbors. If you see something going on that seems wrong, ask them about it, or call your state environmental agency.

Build A Watershed

Create a simple model of a watershed, then observe how runoff and pollutants flow downward in the model.

Objectives:
Observe in miniature how rain flows in a watershed. Define nonpoint source pollution, and watch how it is carried by rain.

Ages:
Primary & Intermediate

Materials:
- *large rectangular pan or basin*
- *heavy-duty aluminum foil or sheet plastic*
- *newspaper or wood blocks*
- *small watering can with shower spout or spray bottle*
- *water*
- *food coloring*
- *loose soil or fine sand*

Subject:
Science

"Go With the Flow" (page 64) explained the concept of watersheds. Now create an action model that shows how they work.

Place blocks or crumpled newspaper in the corners of one end of the pan to make hills. Tear off a piece of aluminum foil slightly larger than the pan. Crumple the foil to make dips and gullies to represent streams, and place it over the blocks, being careful not to tear the foil. (You can use sheet plastic instead, if needed.) At one end, form a basin or pocket to represent a lake that collects water from the tributaries. At the other end, make a valley between the hills. Then prop up that end of the pan slightly. Be sure that the edges of the foil are arranged so that when water is sprayed on it, the water stays in the pan. Pour a little water in the lake. Explain to the class what the model represents, noting that higher elevations or bumps in the foil are land areas, while cracks and dips are bodies of water.

Then students can gently make it "rain" with the watering can or spray bottle. Observe how the water runs off the land into the tributaries and eventually into the lake. Notice how fast water runs off the foil, since it can't soak in, much like it runs off pavement.

Now add "pollution" to the watershed and watch how it travels. First talk about the kinds of pollutants you might find in your watershed: soil, fertilizer, pesticide, paint, oil, and so on. Next add a drop or two of food coloring near the upstream end of the model. Explain that this could be a toxic waste spill, or used motor oil in a storm drain. Ask what the students think will happen to the spill when it rains. Make it rain and watch how the rain carries the pollution downstream into the lake.

Now place a small pile of soil or sand near the stream. Pretend that someone has bulldozed land near a stream and left it bare. Make it rain, and watch how the soil is washed away. Keep it raining until the soil reaches the lake, and let it settle. Explain that this loose soil is called sediment. How is sediment introduced into lakes and ponds? Pass out the "Don't Get Sedimental" Copycat Pages and read them along with the class.

(Adapted from *Waterways: Links to the Sea* by the Maine Coastal Program)

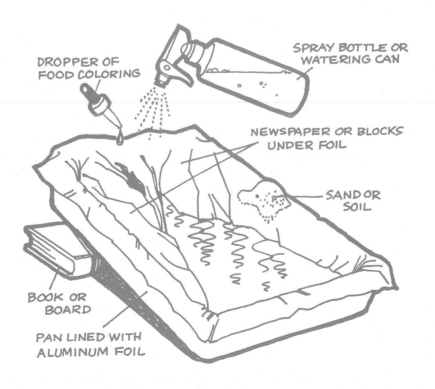

DROPPER OF FOOD COLORING

SPRAY BOTTLE OR WATERING CAN

NEWSPAPER OR BLOCKS UNDER FOIL

SAND OR SOIL

BOOK OR BOARD

PAN LINED WITH ALUMINUM FOIL

PART ONE

PART TWO

RANGER RICK'S NATURESCOPE: POLLUTION—PROBLEMS AND SOLUTIONS

RANGER RICK'S NATURESCOPE: POLLUTION—PROBLEMS AND SOLUTIONS

Grow Green Goo

Create an algae bloom in a jar to see the effect of nutrients on lakes.

Objectives:
Define eutrophication. Grow a culture of algae. Compare the growth rate in two cultures with and without fertilizer.

Ages:
Intermediate and Advanced

Materials:
- *2 gallon jars*
- *tap water, several days old*
- *straw, hay, grass, or algae*
- *plant fertilizer (granular or liquid)*

Subjects:
Science & Math

The story, "Big Stream and Blue Lake" told about *eutrophication*, the process of enrichment with nutrients of a lake or other water body. A major source of nutrients is manmade fertilizer, which is often misused. Homeowners often apply several times the recommended amounts of fertilizer to their lawns and gardens. Farmers may apply fertilizer to saturated ground or in rainy weather, which allows it to run off into waterways, causing algae blooms.

Now create an algae bloom in the classroom by doing an experiment to see how excess fertilizers speed up the growth of algae. Fill each of the two gallon jars with tap water that has been allowed to sit a day or two for chlorine to dissipate. In each jar, place a little mat of straw, hay, grass, or algae. (You can also do this experiment using water from a stream, lake, pond, puddle, or aquarium, eliminating the tap water and mat of straw or other material.)

Calculate the recommended amount of plant fertilizer per gallon, then add twice that amount to one jar; add none to the second (control) jar. Place the jars in a well-lighted area away from drafts or cold air. Record observations on both jars over a month. Add a little more fertilizer to the one jar every 2 weeks.

The jar with fertilizer will eventually grow more algae on the sides and in the water, with slower growth in the non-fertilized control jar. The fertilized jar will support a population of grazing protozoans. Observe the algae and protozoans under a low-powered microscope.

Explain that in real ponds and lakes, it's not just fertilizers that cause eutrophication, but phosphorus and other nutrients from many sources: detergents, excess sediments, oil, and natural sources. While eutrophication is a natural process, it's the increased rate of overfertilizing from human actions that is causing many lakes and ponds to "go green" in a way we'd rather live without.

(Adapted from *Charting our Course* by the Maine Coastal Program and *Environmental Resource Guide: Nonpoint Source Pollution Prevention* by the Tennessee Valley Authority.)

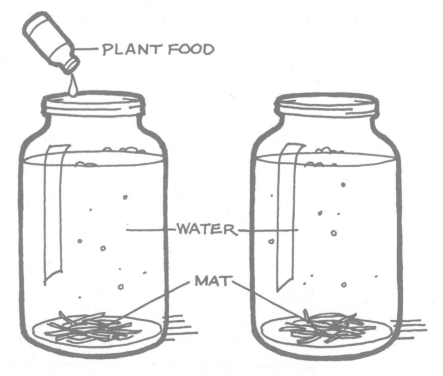

PLANT FOOD

WATER

MAT

Whenever rain falls or snow melts, water flows across farm fields and city streets and washes soil particles, pesticides, pet wastes, oil and other toxic materials into lakes and streams. This process is called *nonpoint source pollution.* The symptoms of nonpoint source pollution are all too familiar: weed-choked lakes, muddy rivers that flood frequently, and an overabundance of carp in our favorite fishing holes.Most nonpoint source pollution is caused by sediments and nutrients; and as you will see, these pollutants can cause serious problems.

Sediments are soil particles eroded from construction sites, streambanks, and cropland. Sediments also include dirt, flakes of metal, and broken pavement washed off city streets. When these particles reach our lakes and streams they do more than turn the water brown.

■ Sediments cause the water to become cloudy, or "turbid," making it difficult for fish to see and feed properly. Sediments can also damage fish gills and impair the feeding and breathing processes in aquatic insects that fish eat.

■ Many fish and aquatic insects lay their eggs on gravel beds. When sediments are deposited on the stream bottom they cover this spawning habitat. They also destroy a stream's natural "riffle and pool" pattern, producing a slow-moving, muddy, less attractive stream.

RANGER RICK'S NATURESCOPE: POLLUTION—PROBLEMS AND SOLUTIONS

■ Muddy or "murky" water contains millions of abrasive soil particles. In moving water these particles can "scour" aquatic plants and animals, removing them from their habitat.

■ Sediment deposits cause streams to become shallower and wider—increasing flooding problems. The shallow water is also heated more efficiently by the sun. This causes water temperatures to rise. Over time, cold water fish, such as trout, are replaced by warm water fish such as carp.

■ Sediments reduce visibility and increase the chances of propellers, rudders and keels running aground or hitting underwater hazards. Swimmers are also affected. Silted swimming areas are undesirable and can be dangerous if deep holes are filled with loose sediment.

■ Sediments cloud the water and cover plant leaves, reducing the amount of sunlight reaching desirable aquatic plants. Sediments also create soft, unstable beds for plant roots. The result is a decrease in food plants available to ducks. Sediment deposits also harm duck populations by filling in wetlands used for breeding.

■ Finally, sediments carry and store toxic materials that can contaminate small organisms. When fish and waterfowl eat the contaminated organisms, the toxins can accumulate in their bodies and cause illnesses, birth defects, and death.

(Text and illustrations adapted with permission from *Brown Water, Green Weeds* by the University of Wisconsin-Extension.)

RANGER RICK'S NATURESCOPE: POLLUTION—PROBLEMS AND SOLUTIONS

Bibliography

(Note: A * at the end of a listing indicates that a book is a good source of pollution pictures.)

GENERAL REFERENCE BOOKS

Blueprint for a Green Planet by John Seymour and Herbert Girardet (Prentice Hall, 1987).
50 Simple Things You Can Do to Save the Earth by Earth Works Project Staff (Earthworks Press, 1995).
Human Impact on the Earth by William B. Meyer (Cambridge University Press, 1996).
Living in the Environment: Principles, Connec-tions and Solutions by G. Tyler Miller, Jr. (Wadsworth, 1996). 9th edition.
Nontoxic Home & Office: Protecting Yourself & Your Family from Everyday Toxics & Health Hazards by Debra L. Dadd (J.P. Tarcher, 1992).
Nontoxic, Natural & Earthwise: How to Protect Yourself & Your Family from Harmful Products & Live in Harmony with the Earth by Debra L. Dadd (J.P. Tarcher, 1990).
People and the Planet: Lessons for a Sustainable Future by Pamela Wasserman (Zero Population Growth, 1996).
Poisoned Land: The Problems of Hazardous Waste by Irene Kiefer (Atheneum Books for Young Readers, 1981).
Pollution Prevention Economics: Financial Impacts on Business and Industry by James R. Aldrich (McGraw Hill, 1996).
The Solution to Pollution: 101 Things You Can Do to Clean Up Your Environment by Laurence Sombke (MasterMedia LTD., 1990).
Toxic Substances in the Environment by Bettina M. Francis (Wiley, 1994).
World Resources 1996-1997: A Guide to the Global Environment by World Resources Institute (Oxford University Press, 1996).
Worms Eat My Garbage by Mary Appelhof (Flowerfield Entertainment, 1982).
Worms Eat Our Garbage: Classroom Activities for a Better Environment by Mary Appelhof (Flowerfield Entertainment, 1993).

CHILDREN'S BOOKS

A Brief Green History of Planet Earth by Ann Fitzpatrick Alper (PPI Publishing, 1996). Intermediate and Advanced
Air Alert: Rescuing the Earth's Atmosphere by Christina G. Miller and Louise A. Berry (Simon & Schuster/Atheneum, 1996). Intermediate and Advanced
Alternative Energy Sources by Gary Chandler and Kevin Graham (21st Century Books, 1996). Intermediate *
Chattanooga Sludge by Molly Bang (Harcourt/Gulliver Green, 1996). Primary and Intermediate
Compost! Growing Gardens from Your Garbage by Linda Glaser (Millbrook Press, 1996). Primary and Intermediate
Earth Book for Kids: Activities to Help Heal the Environment by Linda Schwartz (Learning Works, 1990). Primary and Intermediate
Earth, Fire, Water, Air by Mary Hoffman (Dutton, 1995). Primary and Intermediate
Earth-Friendly Outdoor Fun: How to Make Fabulous Games, Gardens, and other Projects from Reuseable Objects by George Pfiffner (Wiley, 1996). Primary, Intermediate and Advanced
Earth Keepers by Joan Anderson (Harcourt Brace, 1993). Primary and Intermediate
50 Simple Things Kids Can Do to Save the Earth by John Javna et al. (Andrews and McMeel, 1990). Primary, Intermediate and Advanced
Follow that Trash!: All About Recycling by Francine Jacobs (Grosset & Dunlap, 1996). Primary
The Forgiving Air: Understanding Environmental Change by Richard C. Somerville (University of California Press, 1996). Advanced
Garbage by Karen O'Connor (Lucent Books, 1989). Intermediate and Advanced
Hazardous Waste Sites by Kathiann M. Kowalski (Lerner Publications, 1996). Intermediate and Advanced
Imperiled Waters, Impoverished Future: The Decline of Freshwater Ecosystems by Janet N. Abramovitz (Worldwatch Institute, 1996). Advanced
Jack, the Seal and the Sea by Gerald Aschenbrenner (Silver Burdett, 1988). Primary and Intermediate *
Likeable Recyclables by Linda Schwartz (Learning Works, 1992). Primary and Intermediate
The Lorax by Dr. Seuss (Random Books for Young Readers, 1971). Primary and Intermediate
My Earth Book: Puzzles, Projects, Facts & Fun by Linda Schwartz (Learning Works, 1991). Primary
Natural Foods and Products by Gary Chandler and Kevin Graham (21st Century Books, 1996). Intermediate *
Our Poisoned Waters by Edward F. Dolan (Cobblehill, 1997). Intermediate and Advanced
Our Stolen Future by Theo Colborn, Dianne Dumanoski and John Peterson Myers (Dutton, 1996). Advanced
Protecting Our Air, Land, and Water by Gary Chandler and Kevin Graham (21st Century Books, 1996). Intermediate *
The Shoresaver's Handbook: A Citizen's Guide by Tucker Coombe (Lyons and Burford, 1996). Intermediate and Advanced
Taking Care of the Earth: Kids in Action by Laurence Pringle (Boyds Mills, 1996). Intermediate
Trash! by Charlotte Wilcox (Lerner Publications, 1989). Primary and Intermediate *
Water, Water Everywhere: A Book about the Water Cycle by Melvin & Gilda Berger (Children's Books, 1995). Primary
Where Does the Garbage Go? By Paul Showers, part of the Let's-Read-And-Find-Out Science Series (Harper Collins, 1994). Primary and Intermediate

CD-ROM & COMPUTER SOFTWARE

Air Pollution (Advanced) is a program that includes background information, a computer model of air pollution and investigative activities. Write Wards Natural Science Establishment, Inc., PO Box 92912, Rochester NY 14692-9012 or call 1-800-962-2660. Or visit them on the Web at http://www.wardsci.com
Earth Explorer, The Multimedia Encyclopedia of the Environment, CD-ROM (Intermediate and Advanced) by enteractive. This CD-ROM provides an interactive tour of the planet focussing on issues such as acid rain, air quality and wetlands. Displays, charts, graphs and maps link to and support specific topics. To order write Sunburst Communications, 101 Castleton Street, Pleasantville NY 10570-0100 or call 1-800-321-7511.
Earth's Natural Resources CD-ROM (Intermediate and Advanced) by SVE. This CD-ROM contains modules titled "Air, Water, and Soil Resources," "Wildlife Resources," "Energy Resources," and "Future Resources". To order write SVE & Churchill Media, 6677 N. Northwest Highway, Chicago IL 60631 or call 1-800-829-1900. Orders may be faxed to 1-800-624-1678.
Environmental Topics (Intermediate and Advanced) developed by Intentional Educations, Inc. This software program, available in MAC and DOS formats, is a series of interactive tutorials on the topics of energy, waste, global issues, air, water and land. For more information or to order write William Bradford Publishing Company, PO Box 1355, Concord MA 01742 or call 1-800-421-2009.
The Greenhouse Effect and *Thinning of the Ozone Layer* (Intermediate and Advanced) are two titles in the *Mindmap Activity Collections* developed by John Boeschen and Full Circle Media. These software programs designed for the MAC provide information on global warming and the depletion of the ozone layer. For more information or to order write William Bradford Publishing Company, PO Box 1355, Concord MA 01742 or call 1-800-421-2009.*Kids Network Series* by National Geographic Society has several kits applicable to pollution. Titles include *What's in Our Water?, Acid Rain* and *Solar Energy* (all Intermediate). These kits help students perform experiments including water testing, measuring acidity and building solar ovens. Too Much Trash (Intermediate) helps students realize the environmental impact of trash by designing and implementing an in-class trash collection program. To order write National Geographic. Educational Services, PO Box 98018, Washington DC 20090-8018 or call 1-800-368-2728. Orders can be faxed to 1-301-921-1575.
Man and Environment Testbank (Intermediate and Advanced) by MCC Publications. This software program was designed as a resource for teaching environmental studies. Units include *Introduction to Energy, Fossil Fuels, Alternative Energy, Biodiversity,* and others. This program contains over 600 questions, with answers, which are coded to a particular topic so that tests and worksheets can be easily created. Available only in MAC format. For more information or to order write William Bradford Publishing Company, PO Box 1355, Concord MA 01742 or call 1-800-421-2009.
Our Environment CD-ROM (Primary and Intermediate) by Sunburst/Edunetics. This CD-ROM provides information on ways we use our natural resources and the problems associated with using them. Photos, videos, sound and text can be used to build multimedia projects. For more information or to order write Sunburst Communications, 101 Castleton Street, Pleasantville NY 10570-0100 or call 1-800-321-7511.

FILMS, FILMSTRIPS, SLIDE SETS AND VIDEOS

Acid Rain: The Invisible Threat VideoLab (Advanced) includes a videotape or videodisc, that explains acid rain and how it affects lakes, forests and people. A teacher's guide and a 9-station chemistry lab for measuring the effects of acid rain on water, plants, and soils are also included. Video also available separately. For more information or to order write Hubbard Scientific/American Educational Products, Inc., 401 Hickory Street, PO Box 2121, Fort Collins CO 80522.

Cleaning Up Toxics at Home (Intermediate and Advanced) video provides practical information that will help students learn about the hazards in their immediate environment, the everyday products which are dangerous and polluting and what they can do to protect their families and communities. Hazardous waste experts discuss the dangers of many household items and how to properly use and dispose of them. They also suggest less harmful alternatives. A study guide is included. For more information or to order write The Video Project, 200 Estates Drive, Ben Lomond CA 95005 or call 1-800-4-PLANET. Orders can be faxed to 1-408-336-2168.

The Earth At Risk Environmental Video Series (Intermediate and Advanced) has several applicable titles including *Acid Rain, Clean Air, Global Warming* and *Recycling*. To order contact SVE & Churchill Media, 6677 N. Northwest Highway, Chicago IL 60631 or call 1-800-829-1900. Orders may be faxed to 1-800-624-1678.

Emissions and Emotions: Challenges to the European Forests (Intermediate and Advanced) video documents the deadly effect of smokestack emissions on forests in Eastern Europe, Great Britain, Sweden and the Netherlands. To order write Bullfrog Films, PO Box 149, Oley PA 19547 or call 1-800-543-3764.

Energy Efficiency (Intermediate and Advanced) video discusses many improvements in energy efficiency including standards for appliances, automotive fuel and buildings. Breakthroughs in commercial lighting, heating, cooling and ventilation are also covered. A teacher's guide is included. To order write Bullfrog Films, PO Box 149, Oley PA 19547 or call 1-800-543-3764.

Energy Supply (Intermediate and Advanced) video surveys the problems posed by our continuing reliance on conventional energy sources and investigates the possibility of solving those problems through a broader reliance on current renewable energy technologies such as solar power, wind farms, hydro and geothermal power. A teacher's guide is included. To order write Bullfrog Films, PO Box 149, Oley PA 19547 or call 1-800-543-3764.

Films for the Humanities and Sciences has two pollution-related videos. *The Toxic Goldrush* (Intermediate and Advanced, item #1871) and *Down in the Dumps* (Advanced, item #1827). To order write Films for the Humanities and Sciences, Inc., PO Box 2053, Princeton NJ 08543 or call 1-609-275-1400.

Flush Toilet, Goodbye (Advanced) video shows a composting toilet designed by a physicist. The wastewater is cleansed in a pond where waterplants and microbes remove impurities. To order write Bullfrog Films, PO Box 149, Oley PA 19547 or call 1-800-543-3764.

Garbage into Gold (Intermediate and Advanced) video details how recycling can be a business and can create new businesses that benefit not only the environment but also provide job opportunities for people. For more information or to order write The Video Project, 200 Estates Drive, Ben Lomond CA 95005 or call 1-800-4-PLANET. Orders can be faxed to 1-408-336-2168.

Going Green (Intermediate and Advanced) video provides a step-by-step guide to reducing the "un-friendly" impact of household waste on the environment. A guide is included. To order write Bullfrog Films, PO Box 149, Oley PA 19547 or call 1-800-543-3764.

Good Garbage (Intermediate and Advanced) video discusses where things are throw "away" actually go and the importance of the three R's, reduce, reuse and recycle. Examples of reusing and reducing are shown. A discussion guide is included. For more information write Cintia Cabib, 4242 East West Highway, Apt #712, Chevy Chase MD 20815 or call 1-301-657-3225.

Green Means (Intermediate and Advanced) video series has several applicable titles including *Urban Jungle Gets New Spin, Neighborhood Cleanup, Sewage Sanctuary, Solar Ovens* and *Clean AIr Cabs*. To order call Environmental Media at 1-800-368-3382.

Greening Business (Intermediate and Advanced) video discusses how sound environmental practices make good fiscal sense for businesses. To order write Bullfrog Films, PO Box 149, Oley PA 19547 or call 1-800-543-3764.

Hackensack Meadowlands Development Commis-sion has many videos and resource materials, including curriculums, on solid waste and wetlands. Videos include, Dr. Trash (a special with Connie Chung), *The Rotten Truth, Worm Mania* and *The Town that Loved Garbage*. These items are available on loan and some curriculum and resource materials can be photocopied and sent to requestors. For more information write Hackensack Meadowlands Development Commission, Two DeKorte Park Place, Lyndhurst NJ 07071-3799 or call 1-201-460-8300.

Hot Potato (Primary, Intermediate and Advanced) video explores the concepts of waste generation, shared responsibility, incineration, land disposal, groundwater contamination, regulation and "red tape". To order write Bullfrog Films, PO Box 149, Oley PA 19547 or call 1-800-543-3764.

It's Gotten Rotten (Intermediate and Advanced) video provides an introduction to composting. Students will learn how to design an effective compost system for use in their classroom and will see how chemistry and physics play a part in the decomposition process. A teacher's guide is included. To order write Bullfrog Films, PO Box 149, Oley PA 19547 or call 1-800-543-3764.

Keepers of the Coast (Intermediate and Advanced) video explains briefly the water cycle and how rain carries pollution (urban runoff) into the ocean, and how the prevailing swell of the ocean and tides keep this pollution trapped along the coastline. A study guide is included. To order write Bullfrog Films, PO Box 149, Oley PA 19547 or call 1-800-543-3764.

The Murkey Water Caper (Primary) video provides a humorous introduction to water pollution and conservation and gives practical steps that families can take to protect local water sources. A teacher's guide is also included. For more information or to order write The Video Project, 200 Estates Drive, Ben Lomond CA 95005 or call 1-800-4-PLANET. Orders can be faxed to 1-408-336-2168. **National Geographic Society** offers *This World of Energy: II* (Intermediate and Advanced), a series of three filmstrips on energy problems and alternative energies. *Challenges to a Healthy Environment* (Advanced) is a set of two filmstrips: *Hazardous Waste* and *Acid Rain. A First Look at Energy* (Primary) filmstrip explains what energy is, how we use it and why we need to save it. *Earth's Natural Resources: Can They Last?* (Intermediate and Advanced) filmstrip discusses how we rely on natural resources and how we deplete and destroy them. To order write National Geographic Society, PO Box 10597, Des Moines IA 50340 or call 1-800-368-2728.

Natural Waste Water Treatment (Advanced) video features small decentralized sewage treatment facilities which use the natural purifying characteristics of marsh plants. These facilities are operating successfully in Germany, Switzerland and the Netherlands. To order write Bullfrog Films, PO Box 149, Oley PA 19547 or call 1-800-543-3764.

No Time to Waste: Resource Conservation for Hospitals (Advanced) video provides a detailed account of how hospitals reduce the cost of waste material. A study guide and leader's manual are included. To order write Fanlight Productions, 47 Halifax Street, Boston MA 02130.

Once and Future Planet (Intermediate and Advanced) video discusses global warming and the effect our industries and lifestyles have on the earth's atmosphere. A study guide is included. To order write Bullfrog Films, PO Box 149, Oley PA 19547 or call 1-800-543-3764.

Once is Not Enough (Advanced) is a video on glass recycling. To order write Independent Video Services, 401 E. 10th Avenue, Eugene OR 97401 or call 1-800-678-3455.

Opening Your Home to Solar Energy (Intermediate and Advanced) video shows low-cost passive solar options for existing homes, including a simple hot air collector, sun room and south porch. To order write Bullfrog Films, PO Box 149, Oley PA 19547 or call 1-800-543-3764.

Our Future, Our Planet (Intermediate and Advanced) video presents questions, ideas and hope for the future of our planet as discussed by young people who attended the Global Youth Summit in Rio De Janeiro. A teacher's guide is included. For more information or to order write The Video Project, 200 Estates Drive, Ben Lomond CA 95005 or call 1-800-4-PLANET. Orders can be faxed to 1-408-336-2168.

Our Precious Environment (Intermediate) presents the problems of land, air and water pollution and recycling. Available as a set of filmstrips or videos. To order write Educational Images Ltd., PO Box 3456, West Side, Elmira NY 14905 or call 1-800-527-4264. They can also be reached on the web at htpp://www.educationalimages.com For email write edimages@servtech.com

Pointless Pollution: America's Water Crisis (Intermediate and Advanced) discusses the less-recognized cause of water pollution known as nonpoint source pollution, which encompasses all runoff pollution that does not come from a single source (items such as oil, grease, trash, fertilizers and pesticides). A study guide is included. To order write Bullfrog Films, PO Fox 149, Oley PA 19547 or call 1-800-543-3764.

Race for the Future (Intermediate and Advanced) video documents four major competitions for solar and electric cars. A guide is included. To order write Bullfrog Films, PO Box 149, Oley PA 19547 or call 1-800-543-3764.

Recycling is Fun! (Primary) video educates students on the three R's of recycling through visits to a landfill, a recycling center and a supermarket. Students find out ways they can help with our solid waste crisis. A study guide is also included. To order write Bullfrog Films, PO Box 149, Oley PA 19547 or call 1-800-543-3764.

Recycling with Worms (Primary and Intermediate) video shows how organic garbage from one household can be reduced by almost 30% with recycling by using worms. A study guide is included. To order write Bullfrog Films, PO Box 149, Oley PA 19547 or call 1-800-543-3764.

Rethink-Pollution Prevention Pays (Intermediate and Advanced) video emphasizes a fourth "R" to add to "Reduce, Reuse, Recycle", that is "Rethink". Instead of worrying about the after effects of products, attention should be given to developing or changing methods of manufacturing or use so that unnecessary processes or dangerous materials are reduced or eliminated, thereby creating less waste. To order write Bullfrog Films, PO Box 149, Oley PA 19547 or call 1-800-543-3764.

Scrap Dragons (Primary and Intermediate) video shows a young boy teaching his father about recycling scrap metal by touring a local recycling center. For more information or to order call Wave Communications 1-800-892-8433.

Simple Things You Can Do To Save Energy In School (Intermediate and Advanced) video is presented in a how-to format for conserving energy. Many useful ideas could become projects for students. For more information or to order write The Video Project, 200 Estates Drive, Ben Lomond CA 95005 or call 1-800-4-PLANET. Orders can be faxed to 1-408-336-2168.

Spaceship Earth: Our Global Environment (Inter-mediate and Advanced) video helps students understand how their everyday actions have a global impact on our environment. The issues of global warming, ozone depletion and deforestation are made personally relevant. A study guide is also included. For more information or to order write The Video Project, 200 Estates Drive, Ben Lomond CA 95005 or call 1-800-4-PLANET. Orders can be faxed to 1-408-336-2168.

Testing the Waters (Advanced) video discusses the hazardous waste problem in the Niagara River which supplies water to millions of Americans and Canadians. This documentary explains complex concepts at the heart of our hazardous waste problem including "acceptable" levels of toxic chemical exposure, concentrations of toxins in the food chain, risk assessment and the difficulty of choosing a hazardous waste clean-up method. A teacher's guide is included. To order write Bullfrog Films, PO Box 149, Oley PA 19547 or call 1-800-543-3764.

Tina's Journal (Intermediate and Advanced) video depicts a young girl investigating recycling in San Francisco and then establishing a recycling club at her school. For more information or to order write The Video Project, 200 Estates Drive, Ben Lomond CA 95005 or call 1-800-4-PLANET. Orders can be faxed to 1-408-336-2168.

The Trash Troll (Primary) video shows how garbage harms ocean inhabitants and gives children a look at a marine animal hospital caring for injured birds, fish and marine mammals. A study guide is included. To order write Bullfrog Films, PO Box 149, Oley PA 19547 or call 1-800-543-3764.

Troubled Waters: Plastic in the Marine Environ-ment (Intermediate and Advanced) video presents a clear and concise picture of the many ways plastics find their way into our oceans, the danger plastics pose to marine life and the methods used by concerned citizens, government agencies and industry associations to prevent and control the problem. A book is also included. To order write Bullfrog Films, PO Box 149, Oley PA 19547 or call 1-800-543-3764.

Turning the Toxic Tide (Intermediate and Advanced) video depicts the jobs vs. environment conflict and emphasizes that degradation threatens not only the environment but also other jobs. A study guide is included. To order write Bullfrog Films, PO Box 149, Oley PA 19547 or call 1-800-543-3764.

The Underlying Threat (Intermediate and Advanced) video discusses how groundwater is becoming the catch-all for much of our pollution and the consequences for people whose source of drinking water comes from polluted groundwater. A study guide is included. To order write Bullfrog Films, PO Box 149, Oley PA 19547 or call 1-800-543-3764.

Wake Up California! (Advanced) video explains that alternatives to desert landfills are needed for the disposal of nuclear waste. To order call Chip Taylor Communications 1-800-876-2447.

The Wasting of a Wetland (Intermediate and Advanced) video discusses how the Everglades is being threatened by modern industrial pollution, agriculture and development. As the sole source of freshwater for South Florida, wildlife and humans are suffering from the consumption and pollution of this vital resource. A study guide is included. To order write Bullfrog Films, PO Box 149, Oley PA 19547 or call 1-800-543-3764.

The Water in Our Backyard (Advanced) video looks at the national issue of urban water pollution and the ethnic minorities who live, fish and swim there by focusing on the Columbia Slough in Portland OR. For more information or to order write The Video Project, 200 Estates Drive, Ben Lomond CA 95005 or call 1-800-4-PLANET. Orders can be faxed to 1-408-336-2168.

The White Hole (Intermediate and Advanced) video is a commentary on our throw-away society. Helps students learn that there really is no "away" for waste. To order write Bullfrog Films, PO Box 149, Oley PA 19547 or call 1-800-543-3764.

Yosemite and the Fate of the Earth (Intermediate and Advanced) video discusses the many ways the fragile ecosystem of Yosemite is threatened by crowds and pollution. To order write Bullfrog Films, PO Box 149, Oley PA 19547 or call 1-800-543-3764.

Captain Conservation: All About Recycling and ***Captain Conservation: All About Water*** (both Primary) are *Wonders of Learning Kits* by the National Geographic Society. The kits contain a cassette and read-along booklets for 25, ready-to-copy activity sheets and a teacher's guide. For a catalog or to place an order, write to National Geographic, PO Box 11650, Des Moines IA 50340 or call 1-888-647-6733.

Eye on the Environment: Pollution and ***Eye on the Environment: Energy*** (Primary, Intermediate and Advanced) Poster Sets from National Geographic Society includes three posters and a teacher's guide. To order write National Geographic, Educational Services, PO Box 98018, Washington DC 20090-8018 or call 1-800-368-2728. Orders can be faxed to 1-301-921-1575.

OTHER ACTIVITY SOURCES

Living Lightly in the City (An Urban Environmental Education Curriculum) consists of two volumes, one for grades K-3 and one for grades 4-6. Living Lightly on the Planet is available for grades 7-9. These curriculum guides contain activities on exploring urban and suburban surroundings. Write to the Schlitz Audubon Center, 1111 E. Brown Deer Road, Milwaukee WI 53217 or call 1-414-352-2880. Requests can be faxed to 1-414-352-6091.

OBIS (Outdoor Biology Instructional Strategies) offers a "Human Impact" module that includes activities on oil spills, litter, biological pest control and creating nature trails. (Intermediate and Advanced). For more information write to Delta Education, Inc., Box 915, Hudson NH 03051 or call 1-603-889-8899. Or visit them on the Web at http://www.delta-ed.com

Project Learning Tree, sponsored by the American Forest Foundation, has a variety of activities that deal with pollution. For more information write American Forest Foundation, 1111 19th Street, Suite 780, NW, Washington DC 20036 or call 1-202-463-2462.

Project WILD has activities on pollutants. Developed by the Council for Environmental Education. To order write Project WILD, 5430 Grosvenor Lane, Suite 230, Bethesda MD 20814 or call 1-301-493-5447. Visit their web site at http://eelink.umich.edu/wild/

Recycle Today! is the Environmental Protection Agency's program of educational materials on solid waste and recycling for grades K-12. To order call RCRA Information Center at 1-800-424-9346. If within the Washington DC calling area, call 1-703-412-9810. Choose the "Document Order" option from the menu.

Waste: A Hidden Resource is an interdisciplinary curriculum guide for grades 7-12 that includes background information and activities dealing with solid waste. To order write Keep America Beautiful Inc., 1010 Washington Blvd., Stamford CT 06901 or call 1-203-323-8987.

Zero Population Growth, Inc. offers an activity kit titled Counting on People for grades K-6. To order write Zero Population Growth, Inc., 1400 16th Street, NW, Suite 320, Washington DC 20036 or call 1-800-767-1956.

RECYCLED PRODUCTS AND NONTOXIC ALTERNATIVES

Household Product Management Wheel lists alternatives to household toxic materials. To order write Environmental Hazards Management Institute, PO Box 932, Durham NH 03824 or call 1-800-558-3464. Or visit them on the Web at http://www.ehmi.org

Seventh Generation has a catalog of environmentally sound and energy-efficient products. Write Seventh Generation, 360 Interlocken Blvd. Suite 300, Broomfield CO 80021 or call 1-800-456-1177.

SONGS

Recycle Mania is a cassette by Billy B. (Bill Brennan) with six songs about recycling. To order write Do Dreams Music Co., PO Box 5623, Takoma Park MD 20913 or call 1-800-424-5592.

WHERE TO GET MORE INFORMATION

- College and university departments of environmental science or biology
- National Wildlife Federation's (NWF) Conservation Directory (See Acid Rain, Air Quality & Pollution, Greenhouse Effect/Global Warming, Pesticides, Public Health Protection, Pollution Prevention, Solar Energy, Solid Waste Management, Toxicology, Toxic Substances, Water Pollution Management and Water Quality in the Subject Index section)
- NWF's Conservation Directory is the most comprehensive listing of environmental conservation organizations. Each easy-to-read entry contains all the information you need: names, addresses, telephone/fax numbers and description of program areas. The Conservation Directory is a valuable resource tool for people active in the field, students and adults looking for further information on various animal and plant species, and those seeking employment in natural resource management and conservation careers.
- If you want to know the who, what, and where about environmental organizations, this is the book for you. The Conservation Directory can be ordered by

writing to the National Wildlife Federation, 8925 Leesburg Pike, Vienna VA 22184. For discount pricing contact Rue Gordon at (703) 792-4402.
- Magazines such as National Wildlife, International Wildlife, Time, Newsweek, Garbage, E, and others
- State and local departments of solid waste, recycling or public works
- State departments of natural resources
- State EPA offices
- World Wide Web sites:
  Delta Education, Inc. http://www.delta-ed.com
  Educational Images Ltd.
     http://www.educationalimages.com
  EnviroNet http://earth.simmons.edu/
  Environmental Hazards Management Institute
     http://www.ehmi.org
  The Explorer Homepage http://unite2.tisl.ukans.edu/
  National Geographic Society
     http://www.nationalgeographic.com

National Wildlife Federation www.nwf.org
Project WILD http://eelink.umich.edu/wild/
Sunburst Communications
   http://www.SUNBURSTonline.com
Wards Natural Science Establishment Inc.
   http://www.wardsci.com
William Bradford Publishing
   http://www.WKBRADFORD.com

Internet Address Disclaimer:
The Internet information provided here was correct, to the best of our knowledge, at the time of publication. It is important to remember, however, the dynamic nature of the Internet. Resources that are free and publicly available one day may require a fee or restrict access the next, and the location of items may change as menus and homepages are reorganized.

Natural Resources

Ranger Rick® magazine is an excellent source of additional information and activities on many other aspects of nature, outdoor adventure, and the environment. This 48-page award-winning monthly publication of the National Wildlife Federation is packed with the highest-quality color photos, illustrations, and both fiction and nonfiction articles. All factual information in **Ranger Rick** has been checked for accuracy by experts in the field. The articles, games, puzzles, photo-stories, crafts, and other features inform as well as entertain and can easily be adapted for classroom use. To order or for more information, call 1-800-588-1650.

Ranger Rick, *published by the National Wildlife Federation, is a monthly nature magazine for elementary-age children.*

The EarthSavers Club provides an excellent opportunity for you and your students to join thousands of others across the country in helping to improve our environment. Sponsored by Target Stores and the National Wildlife Federation, this program provides children aged 6 to 14 and their adult leaders with free copies of the award-winning **EarthSavers** newspaper and **Activity Guide** four times during the school year, along with a leader's handbook, EarthSavers Club certificate, and membership cards. For more information on how to join, call 1-703-790-4535 or write to EarthSavers; National Wildlife Federation; 8925 Leesburg Pike; Vienna, VA 22184.